Dialogues with Amma

Compiled by
Swami Amritachitswarupananda Puri

Mata Amritanandamayi Center
San Ramon, California, USA

Dialogues with Amma
Compiled by Swami Amritachitswarupananda Puri

Published by:
　Mata Amritanandamayi Center
　P.O. Box 613
　San Ramon, CA 94583-0613, USA

Copyright © 2023 by Mata Amritanandamayi Mission Trust
Amritapuri, Kollam Dt., Kerala, India 690546
All rights reserved.
No part of this publication may be stored in a retrieval system, transmitted, reproduced, transcribed or translated into any language in any form by any publisher.

In India:
　www.amritapuri.org
　inform@amritapuri.org

In Europe:
　www.amma-europe.org

In US:
　www.amma.org

Foreword

Amma, whose very name, Sri Mata Amritanandamayi Devi, Mother of Sweet Bliss, instantly transports us to an ineffable feeling of Love founded on Compassion, Happiness founded on Selfless Service, and Fulfilment founded on God-Realization. In this beautiful book, Swami Amrita-Chit-Swarupananda Puri gives us a first-hand record of some of Amma's most profound teachings - which he has had the great fortune of receiving from Amma during the 30+ years of his residency in Amritapuri Ashram.

These words, given in the form of dialogues with Amma offer rare insight and glimpses into the nature of spirituality and life, re-orienting our purpose of life into seeking and attaining inner peace and fulfillment. In these dialogues, Amma engages with seekers from all walks of life, answering their questions with wisdom, clarity, and compassion. Her teachings are universal and offer guidance for anyone seeking to more deeply understand life's purpose and meaning. She teaches by example that true happiness can only be found within ourselves, and that spiritual practices such as meditation and selfless service are essential to achieving this state.

It is my sincere hope that this book will serve as a source of inspiration and guidance for all those who read it, and that it will help to spread Amma's message of love, compassion, and selfless service throughout the world, ultimately leading us to that state of bliss which is inexplicable.

Dr. P Venkat Rangan
Vice Chancellor
Amrita Vishwa Vidyapeetham
29th September 2023

Introduction

Dialogues with Amma is a book that captures the essence of the spiritual wisdom and teachings of Mata Amritanandamayi Devi, popularly known as Amma, the hugging saint. Amma is a spiritual leader from India who has touched the lives of millions of people around the world through her teachings and example of compassionate in action.

This book features a collection of dialogues between Amma and her devotees on a range of spiritual topics. Amma's teachings are based on the ancient Indian scriptures and emphasize the importance of selfless service, devotion, and the practice of meditation.

Through the conversations in the book, readers can gain insight into the practical application of spiritual principles in everyday life and learn how to cultivate a deeper connection with the divine within themselves. Dialogues with Amma is a treasure trove of spiritual wisdom and inspiration that can guide readers towards a more fulfilling and purposeful life.

Note: These Amma quotes are gathered from amritapuri.org and the Amma Quotes Book. Usually Amma's quotes are self-explanatory, powerful and clear.

Swami Amritachitswarupananda Puri

1. Self
"Children, we are the light of the Divine – the eternally free, infinite and blissful Atman (True Self). Proceed with innocence, effort and faith, and you will discover the bliss of the Self within you." – Amma

2. Bliss
"The purpose of this human birth is to realize our true nature - infinite happiness. Do not miss out on the precious opportunity to find your eternally blissful Self by running after temporary joys." – Amma

3. Self-Enquiry
"Look within, observe the thoughts, and trace them back to their source. Always be convinced, 'I am the nature of Sat-chit-ananda (pure being-awareness-bliss)." – Amma

4. Attitude
"Have the attitude of being a visitor to this world." – Amma

5. Time
"The greatest wealth of a spiritual seeker is time. Without wasting time, with an attitude of surrender, may my children be able to obey the guru's instructions and make their lives meaningful. May grace bless them to achieve this." – Amma

6. Mind
"External success is impermanent. Along with external success, we need inner victory – victory over our mind and senses." – Amma

7. Faith
"Never forget that you are never alone on this journey. God is always with you. Allow Him to take your hand." —Amma

8. Wealth
"In our rush to make as much money as possible, human life is losing its real value." —Amma

9. Self
"There is one truth that shines through all of creation: God is the pure consciousness that dwells in everything." — Amma

10. Peace
"The nature of our inner Self is peace and silence." — Amma

11. Self
"Many people think spirituality is just, 'an outlook' or 'a way of life,' but spirituality is much more than that. It is a deep inquiry into our true self. Real gain comes from the Self alone. If you sincerely inquire within, peace will be gained. Only inquiry into the Self is of eternal value. Only then we shall know 'That' as true bliss." — Amma

12. Devotion
"We have a treasure within us that we will never lose, and that no one can steal. But we will not get it by searching outside. We have to look within. We have to offer the flower of our heart to the Lord." — Amma

13. Selfless Service
"As you help those in need, selfishness will fall away. And, without even noticing it, you will find your own fulfillment." —Amma

14. Meditation
"Meditation is the technique that allows you to shut the doors and windows of the senses, so that you can look within and see your True Self." – Amma

15. Present Moment
"Love is in the present, happiness is in the present, God is in the present. Enlightenment is also in the present. Only the present moment is real. " – Amma

16. World
"In today's world, human beings are dying and human machines are being born in their place." – Amma

17. Grace
"Grace comes out of nowhere. It can happen anytime, in any place." – Amma

18. Enquiry
"The foundation of spirituality is not blind faith. It is enquiry; it is an intense exploration within one's own self." – Amma

19. Mind
"When we have light within, no darkness can affect us." – Amma

20. Attitude
"Happiness depends on how you accept, understand and surrender to situations." – Amma

21. Love
"Logic cuts and divides; Love joins and unites" – Amma

22. Mind
"Human beings are slaves to their thoughts. The mind is a constant flow of thoughts." —Amma

23. Humility
"Only the attitude, 'I am nothing, I know nothing' will help you reach the goal." —Amma

24. Mind
"Concentration stops the flow of thoughts. When thoughts stop, the restless mind ceases its activity." —Amma

25. Devotion
"The real purpose of life is to experience and realize divinity within." —Amma

26. Mind
"In the name of competition, we should not develop feelings of hatred and revenge." —Amma

27. Peace
"Peace of mind is the real wealth." —Amma

28. Mind
"In most cases, worldly love ends in hatred and deep sorrow." —Amma

29. Mind
"With a purified mind, we can feel the pain of others as our own." —Amma

30. Death
"Death is part of life. All of us must face it today or tomorrow. The important thing is not how we die, but how we live." —Amma

31. Awareness
"What you lack is not knowledge, but awareness. If we continuously keep our attention on self-awareness, we will be able to experience peace and happiness." – Amma

32. Prayer
"Pray, 'O Lord, both in happiness and in sorrow, grant me the boon to remember You without fail.'" – Amma

33. Death
"Be like a bird sitting on a dry twig. The bird knows that the twig can break at any moment and is ready to take off at any time." – Amma

34. Compassion
"In times of tragedy, our duty is to lend a helping hand to those in grief and so we light lamps of kindness and compassion." – Amma

35. Mind
"Don't feel bad if someone speaks ill of you. Think that this, too, is for your own good." – Amma

36. Relax
"Whatever you do and wherever you are, relax and you will see how much power you will gain." – Amma

37. Japa
"If you are unable to meditate, chant your mantra or sing bhajans." – Amma

38. Master
"Try to imbibe the Master's teachings and make them part of your life." —Amma

39. Present Moment
"An action always takes place in the present moment. In order to function fully, to be complete and perfect in your actions, you have to learn to live in the present moment."

— Amma

40. Love
"Unconditional love and compassion are expansive, like the sky." —Amma

41. Mind
"Fewer thoughts mean more peace. More thoughts mean less peace and more agitation." —Amma

42. Mind
"The mind is a very effective tool. We can use it to create both hell and heaven." —Amma

43. Anger
"Anger is a weakness; jealousy is a weakness; hatred, selfishness and fear are all weaknesses. The root cause of all of these is the ego." —Amma

44. Life
"Every failure is a lesson for us to learn from." —Amma

45. Nature
"Each and every object in Nature teaches us something. Renunciation and selflessness are the greatest lessons Nature teaches us." – Amma

46. Society
"Today's society overemphasizes skill and has relegated man to the status of mere machines." – Amma

47. Self
"When you fully understand the Supreme Self, the mind won't attach itself to anything external." – Amma

48. Mind
"The more still our mind, the more it begins to resemble the universal mind." – Amma

49. Attachments
"Free from attachments to the past and worries about the future, children express themselves fully." – Amma

50. Mind
"Ask yourself, 'Why do I feel so miserable living in the midst of life's joyful celebration?'" – Amma

51. Love
"Love is the most natural thing for humans. We should perform all our actions from that center point of love." – Amma

52. Mind
"Learn to be considerate. Don't be obsessed with what you think is right." – Amma

53. Mind
"When others get what they wish, we are sad. It's a disease in the mind that eats away our peace." —Amma

54. Attitude
"If your attitude is positive and accepting, you live with God even while busy in the world." —Amma

55. Wealth
"Money is not a problem, but unintelligent attachment to it is." —Amma

56. Charity
"It is through giving that we progress on the spiritual path."
—Amma

57. Compassion
"Consoling a miserable soul, wiping the tears of a crying person is greater than any worldly achievement." —Amma

58. Righteousness
"If you perform your work viewing it as your dharma, your actions become sacred." —Amma

59. Education
"There are two types of education: education for livelihood and education for life." —Amma

60. Nature
"It is the duty of human beings to protect all living creatures, seeing Nature as our mother." —Amma

61. Japa
"Chant your mantra while engaged in work. This way, the mind will be continuously focused on Him." —Amma

62. Behavior
"Keep constant awareness. Make a conscious effort to speak good words and to perform good actions. Practice patience and compassion." —Amma

63. Gratitude
"Thankfulness is a humble, open and prayerful attitude that helps you receive more of God's grace." —Amma

64. Attitude
"Look carefully to see what is of value in others and respect that." —Amma

65. Nature
"By living in harmony with Nature, one gains a healthy mind and body." —Amma

66. Selfless Service
"Purify the mind through selfless service." —Amma

67. Witness
"Develop the ability to stand back as a witness to your thoughts. This will make your mind strong." —Amma

68. Nature
"When humanity serves Nature, Nature serves humanity. When we serve animals and plants, they serve us in return." —Amma

69. Death
"Transcending the cycle of death and rebirth is the real purpose of this life in human form." —Amma

70. Spirituality
"Too much concern about physical security and too little concern about spirituality is the hallmark of today's world." —Amma

71. Creation
"There are no mistakes in God's creation. Every creature and every object that has been created by God is so utterly special." —Amma

72. Faith
"Beauty lies in faith, and faith dwells in the heart. Intellect or reasoning is necessary, but we should not let it swallow up the faith within us. We should not allow the intellect to eat up our heart." —Amma

73. Stillness
"God is in the present moment. The mind attains a state of stillness when it rests in the present moment. That is where perfect peace and bliss are to be found. " —Amma

74. God
"God is not a limited individual who sits alone up in the clouds on a golden throne. God is the pure Consciousness that dwells within everything. Understanding this truth, learn to accept and love everyone equally." —Amma

75. God
"God is not confined to a temple or to any specific place. The Divine is omnipresent, omnipotent and can assume any form. Try to behold your Beloved Deity in everything." —Amma

76. God
"God is not far away from us. It is who we really are, but we need faith to imbibe this truth." —Amma

77. Guru
"The scriptures and the great Masters remind us that the Self, or God, is our true nature." —Amma

78. Love
"Our duty towards God is love and compassion towards the poor and needy." —Amma

79. Wealth
"While many enjoy partying and throwing away their wealth, many others can't even afford a single meal a day."
—Amma

80. God
"We should always maintain the awareness and understanding that no matter what we do, the power behind our actions is God's. Offering your own self into the burning yajna kunda of the infinite power that is God—that is real seva. Atma-samarpanam—offering yourself—is a law of the universe. A few rare individuals live according to this truth. Most are ignorant of it altogether."

81. Feelings
"The thoughts 'I am superior' and 'I am inferior' are both products of the ego." —Amma

82. Master
"The master destroys obstacles and reveals the sacred path to the seeker." —Amma

83. Love
"Divine Love is our true essence." —Amma

84. Parents
"Parents have a great influence on their children. If they are morally good, the children will be good also." —Amma

85. Mind
"The real mistake humans have committed is their inability to differentiate between requirements and luxuries." —Amma

86. Gratitude
"We should try to cultivate an attitude of gratitude. This will help us to earn God's grace. " —Amma

87. Spirituality
"We live in the age of the Internet. Wherever we go on the planet, we need to have the Internet. But, along with an Internet connection, we also need to rediscover our 'Inner-net' connection. Spirituality teaches us how to manage both our internal and external worlds. " —Amma

88. Grace
"Every situation created by the master is a gift of grace, meant to remove the ego." —Amma

89. Amma
"Amma sees everything as part of the whole, as an extension of Her own Self." —Amma

90. Mind
"A porter uses his head to carry luggage. Scientists use their heads to unravel the mysteries of the universe." —Amma

91. Relaxation
"Once you learn the art of relaxation, everything happens spontaneously and effortlessly." —Amma

92. Selflessness
"Learn to place others before yourself. Be considerate of everyone because they are each a doorway to your own Self." —Amma

93. Awareness
"Do your actions with great care and attention and without being consumed by anxiety about the results." —Amma

94. Compassion
"God dwells in the hearts of the compassionate." —Amma

95. Hope
"Always remember that when dusk arrives, it already has dawn in its womb." —Amma

96. Nature
"Mother Earth is always serving us. The sun, the moon and the stars all serve us. What can we do in return for their selfless service?" —Amma

97. Love
"Love and beauty are within you. Try to express them through your actions, and you will definitely touch the very source of bliss." – Amma

98. Enlightenment
"Enlightenment means the ability to recognize oneself in all living creatures." – Amma

99. Mind
"When the waves of the mind subside, you will see that everything you seek is already within you." – Amma

100. Equanimity
"The ability to retain equanimity of mind in all circumstances is what makes a life successful." – Amma

101. Humility
"When you become a zero, you become a hero." – Amma

102. Self
"You own the entire universe. Throw away your begging bowl and look for the treasure hidden within you." – Amma

103. Attitude
"We cannot change situations in life, but we can change our attitude towards them." – Amma

104. Attitude
"A situation becomes a problem only when you interpret it in the wrong way." – Amma

105. Happiness
"Happiness is a decision—a firm decision that 'Whatever comes in life, I will be happy.'" –Amma

106. Pain
"Even painful experiences, when understood deeply, can have a positive effect on our life." –Amma

107. Serving
"Children, never waste an opportunity to serve. The entire world looks up to those who have the heart to do selfless service." –Amma

108. Love
"We are all beads strung together on the same thread of love." –Amma

109. Spirituality
"Spirituality is not an escape from life. It is a choice to turn inwards so that we may know ourselves. Spirituality is the science that teaches us to understand life in greater depth. It is management of the mind" –Amma

110. Equal Vision
"This entire universe is but a play of that cosmic power. Hence, we should see the Mother of the Universe in everything and love and serve everyone equally, without prejudice."

111. Selflessness
"Try to do all your actions as an offering to God. Accept the results as God's will with courage and determination. Incorporate selflessness into your life."

112. True Worship
"The way we serve God's creation expresses our true adoration and worship of God. When we show compassion towards the suffering, we are doing our duty to God."

113. Bliss
"Whereas the momentary happiness obtained from the world ultimately pushes you into the throes of never-ending sorrow, spiritual pain uplifts you to the abode of everlasting Bliss and Peace." –Amma

114. Love
"Even if all the people in the world were to love us, even then, we would not experience an infinitesimal amount of the bliss that we get from God's love." –Amma

115. God's Light
"May we all be able to light the inner lamp within ourselves and bring light to others as well. May everyone have the mental strength to achieve this. May the grace of the Paramatma bless my children."

116. Awareness
"The goal of human life is God-realization. We are not separate from God. A drop of this awareness is already present in us. What we need to do is expand this awareness and strengthen it. We should live every moment with awareness." – Amma

1. Self

"Children, we are the light of the Divine – the eternally free, infinite and blissful Atman (True Self). Proceed with innocence, effort and faith, and you will discover the bliss of the Self within you." – Amma

One day, a group of children from a nearby school came to visit Amma while she was sitting in the courtyard of the Kalari Temple. The children expressed curiosity about the nature of the eternal Atma, the Self, and how to realize it. Amma, with her usual enthusiasm, was delighted to engage with the children and began to share her insights with them.

Amma: Children, do you know what the Atma, the True Self, is?

Children: No, Amma. What is it?

Amma: The Atma is our eternal, unchanging essence. It is who we truly are. This pure consciousness exists within all of us. It is the source of infinite joy and bliss. Do you understand?

Children: Yes, Amma. But how can we experience the bliss of the Atman?

Amma: By turning inward and realizing the true nature of our being—that is how we can experience the bliss of the Atman. This is done through Self-inquiry. Listening, reflecting, and meditating, allow us to uncover the layers of illusion and ignorance that cover up our true nature. When we can do this, we can experience the infinite joy and happiness that is always present within us.

Children: That sounds amazing, Amma. But how do we start on this journey of Self-discovery?

Amma: Start by developing discernment and dispassion, and also cultivate innocence, effort, and faith in yourself and in the Divine. Trust in the process, and be patient with yourself. Remember that you are the light of the Divine, and that the bliss of the Atma is always within you, waiting to be discovered. Keep moving forward with love, kindness, and compassion for yourself and others, and you will surely find your way to the bliss of the Self.

Commentary

Amma teaches that self-realization is the only way to attain real inner happiness. She emphasizes the importance of faith in discovering our true self.

The Light of the Divine

Amma reminds us that we are all reflections of the Divine. We are all connected to the Divine source. In fact, our true nature is divinity. When we recognize this truth, we can see the light of the Divine within us and access it.

The Bliss of the True Self

Amma inspires us to discover the bliss of the true self within. The true self is not limited by the physical body or the ego. It is infinite, eternal, and blissful. When we realize this truth, we can experience profound happiness and fulfillment.

The Importance of Innocence, Effort, and Faith

Amma also highlights the importance of innocence, effort, and faith on our spiritual journey. Innocence allows us to approach the journey with an open mind and heart. Effort reminds us that we must work towards the goal of self-realization. Faith gives us the strength to continue our journey, even when we face challenges.

Conclusion

Through this conversation with the children, Amma encourages us to seek our true nature and to find inner happiness. She reminds us that we are all divine beings, and that we all have the power to access the infinite, blissful nature of the true self within us. By approaching our spiritual journey with innocence, effort, and faith, we can discover the profound bliss of the self.

***

2. Bliss

"The purpose of this human birth is to realize our true nature -- infinite happiness. Do not miss out on the precious opportunity to find your eternally blissful Self by running after temporary joys." – Amma

On a serene day at the beach, Amma arrived for meditation, and Swami joined her. Following their meditation, Amma and Swami engaged in a deep conversation about the subtle nature of true happiness and the nature of the Self as Bliss Absolute. With her characteristic wisdom and insight, Amma emphasized the importance of realizing the true nature of the Self as the source of absolute bliss. She emphasized that we must never overlook this fundamental truth.

Later, Amma and Swami sat in the old hut, as the gentle glow of a lamp cast flickering shadows on the walls. Amma spoke softly, her eyes shining with deep wisdom.

Amma: Swami, have you ever considered the purpose of our human birth?

Swami: Of course, Amma. It is said that our purpose is to achieve liberation from the cycle of birth and death.

Amma: Yes, that is true. But there is a deeper purpose as well. The purpose of our human birth is to realize our true nature as infinite happiness. The Atman, or the true Self, is eternally blissful.

Swami: That is profound, Amma. But how can we discover this blissful Self?

Amma: Through focused effort and faith, we can discover the bliss of the Self within us. We must not miss out on this precious opportunity by running after temporary joys.

Swami: I understand, Amma. But what about the difficulties we face in life? How can we achieve this realization amidst the struggles of the world?

Amma: We must proceed with innocence and effort, with a deep faith in the Divine. By remaining steadfast in our practice, we can achieve the ultimate goal of Self-realization.

Swami nodded, his eyes filled with a sense of purpose and understanding. The two sat in silence for a few moments, as the lamp gently flickered in the background. They both knew that the journey ahead would be long and challenging, but with Amma's guidance, Swamiji felt a newfound sense of hope and determination.

Commentary

In this conversation, Amma emphasizes the importance of realizing our true nature. She exhorts us not get caught up in temporary pleasure. Her words highlight the significance of using our human birth for the highest purpose and finding infinite happiness within ourselves.

The Purpose of Human Birth

Amma reminds us that the purpose of our human birth is to realize our true nature. We are not here to merely pursue temporary joys and material possessions. Instead, we must use this precious opportunity to discover our infinite and eternal nature.

The Danger of Temporary Joys

Here, Amma warns against getting caught up in temporary pleasures. These temporary pleasures are fleeting and cannot provide lasting happiness. If we focus too much on temporary joys, we may miss out on the opportunity to discover our true nature and experience infinite happiness.

Finding the Eternally Blissful Self

Amma emphasizes that we can find infinite happiness within ourselves by realizing our true nature. Our true nature is not limited by the physical body or the material world. It is eternal and infinite. When we realize this truth, we can experience profound and lasting happiness.

Conclusion

Amma's words inspire us to use our human birth for the highest purpose. She encourages us to look beyond temporary joys and to seek infinite happiness within ourselves. By realizing our true nature, we can experience a profound and lasting happiness that cannot be found in the material world.

***

3. Self-Enquiry

"Look within, observe the thoughts, and trace them back to their source. Always be convinced, 'I am the nature of Sat-chit-ananda (pure being- awareness-bliss)." –Amma

As the sun began to set on the horizon, Amma was singing devotional bhajans in the peaceful atmosphere of the Kalari. After the bhajans finished, Swami expressed curiosity about the path to realizing the Self amidst the tumultuous tides of thoughts that so often distract us from our inner truth. The tranquil, awe-inspiring sunset provided the perfect backdrop for their conversation, as they explored the challenges the mind creates and discussed ways to navigate through them to reach the infinite potential within.

Amma: Swami, do you ever take the time to look within and observe your thoughts?

Swami: Yes, Amma, I do my best to practice self-reflection and observe my thoughts.

Amma: That's wonderful. It's important to trace your thoughts back to their source and always remember that you are the nature of Sat-Chit-Ananda, pure Being-Awareness-Bliss.

Swami: But Amma, how can I be sure of that? At times, I still experience negative thoughts and emotions.

Amma: It's natural to experience negative thoughts and emotions, but they are not your true nature. By observing them and tracing them back to their source, you can become convinced of your true nature as Sat-Chit-Ananda. It takes effort and practice, but the rewards are infinite happiness and peace.

Swami: Thank you, Amma. Your words always light up my spiritual practice with clarity and inspiration.

Commentary

To know the Atma, the nature of our Self, it is essential to understand that in every experience, 'I am there.' I am the one knowing. This knowledge precedes all of our experiences. This means that 'I am' is the very basis from which all experiences are happening; it is the source from which all experiences are known.

Therefore, 'I am' is the 'Beingness,' the 'Knowingness' that remains unchanged in all experiences. In other words, the content and substratum of all experiences is 'Knowingness-Beingness,' just like water is the substratum and content of waves. This indicates that our nature, and the nature of everything, is 'Knowingness-Beingness' without any change, which is absolutely blissful in nature.

In the body-mind-world complex, many changes occur continuously, but the Self remains unchanged. That's why it is immortal in nature. The Self is not affected by any changes that occur.

Thus, to know the Atma, one must focus on the 'I am' aspect of oneself, which is the fundamental and unchanging aspect of all experiences. By recognizing the 'I am' as 'Beingness-Knowingness,' one can come to understand the nature of the Self as immortal, unchanging, and blissful.

Thus, the nature of the Self, or Atma, is pure Consciousness, pure Knowingness, which is the fundamental and unchanging aspect of all experience. The Self is not affected by any changes that occur in the body-mind-world complex, and its nature is always that of 'Knowingness-Beingness.' By recognizing the 'I am' aspect of oneself and understanding this as the source and substratum of all experiences, one can come to realize the nature of the Self as immortal, unchanging, and blissful. This understanding leads to the ultimate goal of Advaita philosophy, which is the realization of the oneness of the Self and the Absolute.

4. Attitude
"Have the attitude of being a visitor to this world." – Amma

Sadhu: Amma, I am feeling so lost and helpless. The mafia has taken over my ashram in Haridwar. I have devoted my entire life to serving God, and now I have nowhere to go.

Amma: My child, I am sorry to hear about what happened to your ashram. But remember, we are only visitors to this world. We cannot control what happens in it, but we can control our attitude towards it.

Sadhu: But how can I stay positive when everything I have worked for has been taken away from me?

Amma: It's not about being positive or negative, my child. It's about having the attitude of a visitor. When we visit someone's house, we don't get attached to their belongings because we know we will eventually have to leave. Similarly, when we understand that this world is not our permanent home, we won't get attached to the things that happen to us.

Sadhu: I see what you mean, Amma. But how can I cultivate this attitude?

Amma: Through spiritual practice, my child. Meditation, Self-inquiry, and surrender to God can help you realize your true nature as Sat-Chit-Ananda, pure Being-Awareness-Bliss. When you realize that, you will see everything in this world as a passing show, and your inner peace will not be disturbed by external events.

Sadhu: Thank you, Amma!

Amma: Remember, my child, the divine is always with you, and nothing can ever take that away.

Commentary
Amma encourages us to adopt the attitude of a visitor in this world. Her words remind us of the importance of detachment and reminds us that our time on this earth is temporary.

Detachment

Amma consistently emphasizes the importance of detachment. When we adopt the attitude of being a visitor, we remember that we are here temporarily. This awareness can help us let go of material attachments and possessions, so we can focus on what truly matters.

Impermanence

Amma also emphasizes the impermanence of life. Nothing in this world is permanent, and everything is subject to change. By adopting the attitude of a visitor, we can recognize the impermanence of life and focus on what is important in the long term.

Mindfulness

This conversation encourages us to be mindful of our time on this earth. When we adopt the attitude of a visitor, we are reminded to make the most of our time here and to focus on what truly matters.

Conclusion

Amma's words remind us to adopt the attitude of a visitor in this world. By doing so, we can cultivate detachment, recognize the impermanence of life, and be more mindful in how we use our time here.

***

5. Time

"The greatest wealth of a spiritual seeker is time. Without wasting time, with an attitude of surrender, may my children be able to obey the guru's instructions and make their life meaningful. May grace bless them to achieve this." – Amma

Amma noticed that one of her brahmachari disciples was spending too much time in idle chatter and gossip. She called him over and spoke to him with concern in her eyes.

Amma: My child, I see that you spend a lot of time engaging in gossip with others. Don't you understand the value of time for a spiritual seeker?

Brahmachari: Well, Amma, I suppose I haven't thought about it much. I just like spending time with my friends and having fun.

Amma: Of course, it's natural to want to spend time with friends and have fun. But as a spiritual seeker, time is your most valuable asset. It's the greatest wealth you have.

Brahmachari: I see what you mean, Amma. But how can I use my time more effectively?

Amma: By cultivating an attitude of surrender and obedience to your guru's instructions, you can make your life more meaningful. This means using your time wisely, without wasting it on trivial matters like gossip.

Brahmachari: Thank you, Amma. I promise I will try to be more mindful about how I spend my time. I promise to focus more on spiritual pursuits.

Amma: May grace bless you to achieve this, my child. Remember, time is precious, and we must use it wisely on the path of spiritual growth.

Commentary

In this conversation, Amma highlights the importance of time for spiritual seekers. Her words emphasize the significance of surrendering to the guru's instructions and making our lives meaningful.

Time as a Valuable Resource

Amma reminds us that time is the most valuable resource for spiritual seekers. The time we have in this world is limited, and it is important to use it wisely. By using our time effectively, we can make progress on our spiritual journey and achieve our goals.

The Importance of Surrender

Amma also emphasizes the importance of surrendering to the guru's instructions. The guru is a spiritual guide who can help us on our journey to self-realization. By surrendering to the guru's instructions, we can receive guidance and support on our journey.

Making Life Meaningful

Amma's words encourage us to make our lives meaningful. By using our time effectively and surrendering to the guru's instructions, we can make progress on our spiritual journey and create purpose and meaning in our lives.

Conclusion

Amma reminds us here of the importance of time and surrender in making our lives meaningful. As spiritual seekers, it is essential to use our time wisely and to follow the guidance of our guru, so we can make progress on our journey. By doing so, we can achieve our goals and find purpose and meaning in our lives. May grace bless us to achieve this.

6. Mind

"External success is impermanent. Along with external success, we need inner victory – victory over our mind and senses."
– Amma.

One evening, as the sky was painted with shades of red and gold, Amma engaged in a heart-to-heart conversation with a brahmachari who was feeling lost and uncertain on his spiritual path. As they sat together on the beach, the brahmachari opened up saying...

Brahmachari: Amma, I am feeling lost and unsure about my spiritual path. I don't know what I should do.

Amma: Don't worry, my child. Sometimes we can feel lost, but it is important to remember that we are always on the right path, as long as we are seeking the truth.

Brahmachari: But how do I know if I am on the right path?

Amma: The right path is the one that leads you towards inner peace and happiness. If you feel calm and content, even in the face of challenges, then you are on the right path.

Brahmachari: I see. But what can I do to find inner peace and happiness?

Amma: You can start by cultivating devotion and practicing meditation. Devotion is the key to unlocking the door to the heart, and meditation is the key to calming the mind and connecting with the Divine within you.

Brahmachari: I understand. But what about the distractions and temptations of the world? How can I resist them?

Amma: It is important to practice self-discipline and to stay focused on your goal. Remember, external success is impermanent. Along with external success, we need inner victory - victory over our mind and senses. This inner victory is the key to lasting happiness and fulfillment.

Brahmachari: Thank you, Amma.

Amma: My child, I am always here to guide and support you on your spiritual journey. Just keep your heart open, and the Divine will show you the way.

Commentary

In response to this bramachari's sincere question, Amma shares profound insights, emphasizing the importance of inner victory over external success. Her words highlight the significance of achieving control over our mind and senses.

Impermanence of External Success

Amma reminds us that external success is impermanent. Material possessions, wealth, and fame are all temporary and subject to change. True happiness and fulfillment cannot be found in external success alone.

Victory over Mind and Senses

Amma further emphasizes the importance of achieving victory over our mind and senses. Our mind and senses can be a source of distraction that can lead us away from our true purpose. By achieving control over our mind and senses, we can focus on our spiritual journey and find inner peace and happiness.

The Importance of Inner Victory

While external success can bring temporary happiness, true and lasting happiness can only be found within. By achieving inner victory, we can find a profound sense of fulfillment and purpose in our lives.

Conclusion

This conversation between Amma and the bramachari reminds us of the impermanence of external success and emphasizes the importance of achieving inner victory. By achieving control over our mind and senses, we can focus on our spiritual journey and find true happiness and fulfillment there. External success may bring temporary happiness, but true and lasting happiness can only be found within.

***

7. Faith

"Never forget that you are never alone on this journey. God is always with you. Allow Him to take your hand." – Amma

A devotee who had lost his mother came to Amma, feeling sad and unsure about what to do next. Amma listened compassionately as he poured out his heart, and then spoke these words of wisdom.

Devotee: Amma, I just lost my mother, and I'm feeling so alone. I don't know what to do next.

Amma: My child, I understand your pain. It is natural to feel alone and lost when we lose someone dear to us. But always remember, you are never alone on this journey. God is always with you, holding your hand and guiding you.

Devotee: How do I allow God to take my hand, Amma? I'm feeling so lost and disconnected.

Amma: Through prayer, meditation, and surrender, my child. Trust that God knows what is best for you, and have faith that He will guide you in the right direction. Let go of your worries and fears, and allow God's love and grace to fill your heart. Remember, you are a child of God, and He will never abandon you.

The devotee bowed his head in gratitude.

Amma: My dear child, always remember that God's love and grace are infinite. You are never alone, and He will always be there to guide and support you on your journey. Trust in His plan, and everything will fall into place.

Commentary

Amma reminds us that we are never alone on our journey, that God is always with us. We need only surrender to God and allow Him to guide us.

The Presence of God:

God is always with us. We are never truly alone on our journey. God is always there to guide us and support us. By inviting

God's presence through prayer, we can find comfort and strength in difficult times.

Surrendering to God

When we surrender to God, we allow Him to guide us and help us on our journey. Surrendering to God can bring us a sense of peace and freedom from worry and anxiety.

Allowing God to Guide Us

If we trust in God's guidance and allow Him to take our hand and guide us, purpose and direction will come. The ups and downs of life will become manageable, and we will be able to focus on our spiritual journey.

Conclusion

In this conversation, Amma reminds us that we are never alone on our journey, that God is always with us. By surrendering to God, and allowing Him to guide us, we can find comfort, peace, and purpose.

***

8. Wealth

"In our rush to make as much money as possible, human life is losing its real value." —Amma

Once, a man came to Amma with tears in his eyes. He had lost his business after taking a shortcut to make more money, which led him into a trap. Amma spoke to him and said…

Amma: My son, what's wrong?

Man: Amma, I am in so much pain. I lost my business, my savings, everything. I was so focused on making more and more money that I forgot about the real value of life.

Amma: My child, I am sorry to hear about your loss. But remember, the real value of life cannot be measured in money. In our rush to make as much money as possible, we forget about the simple things that bring us true happiness.

Man: But Amma, how can I survive without money? I need it to pay my bills and take care of my family.

Amma: Of course, my child, money is important for our basic needs. But we must not forget the bigger picture. Money is just a means to an end, not the end itself. Focus on the things that truly matter in life, like love, compassion, and service to others.

Commentary

Amma draws attention to the fact that in our pursuit of wealth, we are losing sight of the true value of human life. Her words emphasize the importance of putting human life first and recognizing that as true wealth.

The Pursuit of Wealth

Amma's words cast a spotlight on the modern-day obsession with money and material possessions. We are often so caught up in the pursuit of wealth that we overlook life's true value.

The Real Value of Human Life

Human life is precious and should be treated with respect and dignity. Each individual has inherent value, regardless of their material possessions or social status.

The Need to Prioritize What is Really Important

Amma encourages us to prioritize human life over material possessions. In our pursuit of wealth, we should not overlook the inherent dignity of human life. We should strive to create a society that values each human life and treats each individual with respect and dignity.

Conclusion

We should not lose sight of the inherent value of each person, regardless of their material possessions or social status. By prioritizing human life over material possessions, we can create a more compassionate and just society.

***

9. Self

"There is one truth that shines through all of creation. God is the pure consciousness that dwells in everything." – Amma

Once an IAS officer from Orrisa came to Amma, as his spirituality had taken a hit. He was feeling depressed that he was not able to experience the non-dual truth. He approached Amma and asked:

IAS Officer: Amma, I have been studying spirituality and practicing meditation for years now, but I still cannot feel the non-dual truth. Can you guide me?

Amma: The non-dual truth is that there is only one reality, which is God, the pure consciousness that dwells in everything. It is not something that can be explained through words, but rather something that can be experienced through direct realization.

IAS Officer: But how can I experience this truth?

Amma: By turning your attention inward, you can begin to witness the presence of God within you. With the regular practice of meditation, you can begin to cultivate a deep awareness of this truth and feel it in every moment of your life.

IAS Officer: But how do I know that this is the truth?

Amma: The truth can only be known through direct experience. It is not something that can be proven or disproven through intellectual debate or analysis. You must trust your own experience and intuition and have faith that the truth will reveal itself to you in its own time.

Commentary

Amma highlights the idea that God is present in everything and everyone. Her words emphasize the importance of experiencing pure consciousness and the interconnectedness of all things.

The Presence of God
God is present in everything, He dwells within all of creation. If we want to experience this divine presence, however, we must strive to see it within ourselves and in the world around us.

Pure Consciousness
In this conversation, Amma hones in on pure consciousness, that state of awareness that is free from the ego and the material world. This state of awareness can gradually be realized through meditation, self-inquiry, and other spiritual practices.

Interconnectedness
Amma also emphasizes the interconnectedness of all things. If God is present in everything, then everything is interconnected and part of a larger whole. This interconnectedness reminds us that we are all part of a larger spiritual journey and that our thoughts and actions have an impact on the world around us.

Conclusion
Amma's reminds us that God is present in everything and everyone. Pure consciousness is spiritual enlightenment, which is experienced as the interconnectedness of all things. By recognizing the presence of God within us, and in the world around us, we can deepen our spiritual awareness and live a more compassionate and connected life.

***

10. Peace
"The nature of our inner Self is peace and silence."
– Amma.

A spiritual seeker from Ranchi, one of Yogananda's Ashrams, once came to Amma with worries that he was not progressing, even though he was meditating eight hours straight every day. He finally decided to ask Amma for guidance.

Amma: Welcome, my child. What brings you here?

Spiritual Seeker: Amma, I have been practicing meditation for eight hours a day at Yogananda's Ashram in Ranchi, but I am not progressing. I am still unable to find peace and silence within myself.

Amma: My child, the nature of our inner Self is peace and silence. But the mind is restless and difficult to control. You need to have faith in your practice and continue with patience and determination.

Spiritual Seeker: But Amma, I have been practicing for so long, and still, I feel no progress.

Amma: The practice of meditation is not about achieving something. It is about letting go and surrendering to the present moment. Do not worry about progress or attainment. Just be present with the practice, and eventually, the peace and silence you seek will reveal themselves.

Spiritual Seeker: Thank you Amma.

Amma: Remember, my child, the journey to the Self is not easy, but it is worth it. Keep practicing with faith, and you will find what you seek.

Commentary

In this conversation, Amma emphasizes the peaceful, silent nature of the inner Self. Her words point to the importance of accessing this inner peace and recognizing its true nature.

The Inner Self

Amma's words reminds us that our true nature does not abide in the ego or the material world. Rather, our true nature is the inner Self, which is pure and unchanging. By accessing this inner Self, we can find peace and fulfillment in our lives.

The Nature of Inner Self

The nature of the inner Self is peace and silence. This peace and silence are not dependent on external circumstances or material possessions. Instead, they are the inherent nature of the inner Self.

Accessing Inner Peace

Amma encourages us to experience this inner peace by quieting our minds and turning inward. Through meditation, mindfulness, and other spiritual practices, we can cultivate a sense of inner peace and connect with our own true nature.

Conclusion

Amma's compassionate words remind us all to make sincere efforts to realize our inner Self. By reawakening to this, we can find pure peace and perfect fulfillment in our lives. With this goal in mind, we must persevere with our meditation and mindfulness practices.

***

11. Self

"Many people think spirituality is just, 'an outlook' or 'a way of life,' but spirituality is much more than that. It is a deep inquiry into our true self. Real gain comes from the Self alone. If you sincerely inquire within, peace will be gained. Only inquiry into the Self is of eternal value. Only then we shall know 'That' as true bliss." – Amma

A group of young boys were gathered in front of Amma, expressing their desire to join her Ashram and embark on a path of sadhana, spiritual practice. They were seeking guidance from Amma about what spiritual practice entails and how to approach it. Amma responded by explaining that spirituality is not just an outlook or a way of life, but a deep inquiry into one's true self. She emphasized the importance of self-inquiry, stating that it is the only path to eternal peace and true bliss. The boys listened attentively, eager to learn more about the path of sadhana and how to incorporate it into their lives.

Amma: Welcome, my dear boys. I am glad to see your interest in spirituality and your willingness to do sadhana. Can you tell me what brings you here?

Boy 1: Amma, we are tired of leading materialistic lives and want to explore the spiritual path. We want to learn and practice sadhana to attain inner peace and happiness.

Amma: That's wonderful to hear! But remember, spirituality is not just an outlook or a way of life, it is a deep inquiry into our true self. Real gain comes from the Self alone. If you sincerely inquire within, peace will dawn. Only inquiry into the Self is of eternal value. We should know 'That' as the true bliss.

Boy 2: Amma, we are ready to join your ashram and do sadhana. Can you guide us on what kind of sadhana we should do?

Amma: There are different paths to reach the ultimate goal of self-realization. My dear boys, choose the path that suits your temperament and follow it with dedication and surrender. The key is to remember that sadhana is not just about practicing meditation or yoga for a few hours a day. It's about living a spiritual life, where every action, every thought, and every emotion is infused with spirituality.

Boy 3: Amma, we are ready to make that commitment. Can you please guide us on how we can integrate spirituality into our daily life?

Amma: It's good to see your enthusiasm. The first step is to cultivate the right attitude towards life. Remember that the nature of our inner self is peace and silence. So, try to maintain that inner peace amidst the outer chaos. The second step is to practice selfless service, or seva, as it helps to purify our mind and heart. And finally, always remember that God is with you, my dear boys, guiding and protecting you every step of the way.

Commentary

Amma highlights the importance of spirituality as a deep inquiry into our true selves. Her encouraging words emphasizes that real peace comes through inquiry into the Self.

Spirituality as Inquiry

Amma further emphasizes that spirituality is not just an outlook or a way of life, but a deep inquiry into our true selves. This inquiry involves a vigorous and sincere questioning of our beliefs, values, and assumptions. If done sincerely, it leads to a deep understanding of ourselves and our place in the world.

Real Gain from the Self

Amma's words remind us that real gain comes from the Self alone. By turning inward and exploring our true nature, we can find unlimited peace and fulfillment in our lives. Real gain is never dependent on external circumstances or material possessions.

Inquiry into the Self

Amma lovingly repeats that only inquiry into the Self is of eternal value. By exploring our true nature, we can gain a deeper understanding of ourselves and our connection to the world around us. This inquiry can lead to an incomparable sense of peace and fulfillment that cannot be found in external pursuits.

Conclusion

Amma's words give a crystal-clear definition of spirituality as a deep inquiry into our true selves. By exploring our true nature and turning inward, we can find peace and fulfillment. Real profit comes from the Self alone. In fact, inquiry into the Self is like a fixed deposit that never loses value.

***

12. Devotion

"We have a treasure within us that we will never lose, and that no one can steal. But we will not get it by searching outside. We have to look within. We have to offer the flower of our heart to the Lord." – Amma

Amma was sitting in a hut with a group of householders who had come to ask about the best way to reach God. One of them lovingly put this question to Amma:

Householder 1: Amma, what is the best way for us to reach God?

A brilliant smile lit up Amma's face.

Amma: Daughter, the best way to reach God is by looking within ourselves. We have a treasure of divine love and wisdom within us. It is our birthright to claim it. But we must remember that it cannot be found by searching outside. We have to turn our attention inward, and offer the flower of our heart to the Lord. This means surrendering our ego and selfish desires, and opening ourselves up to the infinite love and grace of the Divine.

Householder 2: But Amma, it can be hard to find the time and motivation to do spiritual practices like prayer and meditation. What can we do to stay on track?

Amma: It is true that the path to God requires discipline and dedication. But it is also important to remember that every moment of our lives can be a spiritual practice, if we approach it with the right attitude. Whether we are cooking a meal, tending to our family, or doing our job, we can offer it all up as service to the Divine. If we live our lives with love and compassion, with the intention of serving others, we will naturally be drawn closer to God."

Householder 3: Amma, how can we know if we are making progress on the spiritual path?

Amma: Progress on the spiritual path cannot be measured by external achievements or by how many hours we spend in meditation. The true measure of progress is the degree to which we have let go of our ego and our attachment to the material world, the degree to which we have opened ourselves up to the infinite love and wisdom of the Divine. This is a gradual process, and we must have patience and persistence. But if we continue to offer the flower of our heart to the Lord, we will surely see progress."

Commentary

In this conversation with householder devotees, Amma stresses the importance of offering our hearts to the Lord.

The Treasure Within

Amma's words reiterate the idea that we all have a treasure within us that no one can steal. This treasure is not made up of material possessions or external accomplishments, but of something much more deep and profound.

Looking Inside

Amma emphasizes the importance of looking inside to find this treasure. We cannot find it by searching outside or relying on external circumstances.

Offering Our Hearts to the Lord

Amma encourages us to offer the flower of our heart to the Lord by surrendering to a higher power and cultivating a sense of devotion and love.

Conclusion

Amma lovingly reminds us of the treasure that lies within us and of the need to look within to find it. By turning inward and offering our hearts to the Lord, we can connect with our true nature and find the treasure that no one can steal. When a sense of devotion, love and surrender to the Divine awakens within us, we draw closer to this treasure.

***

13. Selfless Service

"As you help those in need, selfishness will fall away. And, without even noticing it you will find your own fulfillment."

– Amma

On December 26, 2004, a devastating Tsunami struck the ashram and the surrounding villages, leaving many people with nothing but loss and grief. In this time of desperate need, Amma responded. She gathered all the bramacharis and residents of the ashram and inspired them to help those affected by the disaster.

As the ashram residents all gathered around Amma, one of the bramacharis boldly asked...

Bramachari: Amma, why should we help others? What's in it for us?

Amma smiled compassionately.

Amma: My dear child, helping others is not just about doing a good deed or being kind. It is about recognizing that we are all connected, that we are all part of one human family. When we help others, we are helping ourselves because our selfishness and ego begin to fall away. By helping others, without even noticing, we find our own fulfillment and happiness. When we help those in need, we are serving God. It is through serving others that we serve the divine. So, let us all work together to help those affected by the Tsunami. Let us offer our hands, our hearts, and our resources to all those who need them. In doing so, we will find that we have helped ourselves as well.

Brahmachari: How is that possible, Amma?

Amma: When we help those in need, we develop empathy and compassion towards them. We begin to see ourselves in them, and in turn, selfishness falls away.

Brahmachari: I see, Amma.

Amma: And as we continue to help others, without even noticing, we will find our own fulfillment. It is like a boomerang effect.

Brahmachari: Now I understand, Amma.

Amma: Remember, we are all connected. The joy and suffering of one affects us all. By helping others, we are contributing to the greater good and creating a positive ripple effect in the world. And remember, my dear child, helping others is not just an act of kindness, it is also a way to help ourselves.

Commentary

In this extraordinary conversation, Amma highlights the connection between helping others and finding fulfillment. Her words emphasize the importance of selflessness and the rewards that come from helping those in need.

Helping Those in Need

Amma teaches that by helping others, we can make a positive impact on the world and bring comfort and support to those who are struggling.

Selflessness

Her words remind us that it is when we focus on helping others that we are able to let go of our own selfish desires and concerns. Such selflessness inevitably brings a sense of peace and fulfillment that cannot be found in the glittering seashells of the world.

Finding Fulfillment

Without even noticing its transformative power, service to others brings a sense of purpose and joy. Ironically, when we help others, it is we ourselves who find a sense of fulfillment—the fulfillment that comes from making a positive impact on the world.

Conclusion

Amma's words reminds us of the importance of helping others and cultivating a sense of selflessness. By focusing on the needs of others, we find a sense of fulfillment that cannot be found in external pursuits. When we choose to make a positive impact on the world, we find a sense of joy and purpose. By helping others, we are helping to create a more compassionate and just society, while finding a deep sense of fulfillment in our own lives.

***

14. Meditation

"Meditation is the technique that allows you to shut the doors and windows of the senses, so that you can look within and see your True Self." – Amma

Meditation is a powerful technique that has been used for centuries to help spiritual seekers connect with their inner selves to find peace and clarity. It is a practice that helps to quiet the mind, so we can let go of external distractions and tap into the infinite wisdom and knowledge that lies within.

Once a swami from Haridwar approached Amma to ask about meditation.

Swami: Amma, I have been meditating for many years. Once I experienced nirvikalpa samadhi, but since then, I have not been able to reach that state again. What should I do?

Amma: My dear son, you must understand that you are always in that state of oneness-- you are That. Meditation is not about achieving a certain state or experience; it is a tool to help you realize the truth of your being.

Swami: But how can I become this truth?

Amma: Through continuous practice of meditation, you can learn to quiet the mind and let go of all thoughts and distractions. By doing so, you can experience the pure awareness and presence that is always within you. This is the essence of meditation and the path to self-realization.

Swami: Amma, can you explain the purpose of meditation?

Amma: Son, meditation allows you to shut the doors and windows of the senses, so that you can turn your attention inward and see your True Self. It is through this process of inner exploration that we can begin to understand the nature of our mind, and the true essence of who we are.

Swami: But how can I shut the doors and windows of the senses?

Amma: Through consistent practice and dedication you can learn to quiet the mind and let go of all external distractions. By turning your attention inward, you will be able to cultivate deep inner peace and stillness. This will help you to connect with your True Self. Remember, meditation is not about achieving a particular state or experience, but rather, it is a process of inner transformation and self-discovery.

Commentary

In this dialogue, Amma highlights the importance of meditation. It is a powerful technique that helps us to look within and connect with our True Self. To experience this Self, we must shut out all external distractions and abide within.

The Importance of Meditation

Amma clearly defines meditation as a way to look within and connect with our True Self. By quieting the mind and shutting out external distractions, we can know our inner being and find a sense of peace and clarity.

Shutting the Doors and Windows of the Senses

Amma stresses that it is essential to shut the doors and windows of the senses during meditation. This means letting go of external distractions and turning inward to focus on our inner being.

Connecting with the True Self

As we come in contact with our inner being in meditation, we find the purpose, clarity, and fulfillment that can never be found in external pursuits.

Conclusion

By shutting out external distractions and turning inward, we find a sense of peace and clarity that help us navigate the challenges of life. By practicing meditation, we slowly come to know our True Self.

Dialogues with Amma

***

15. Present Moment

"Love is in the present, happiness is in the present, God is in the present. Enlightenment is also in the present. Only the present moment is real." – Amma.

A westerner sat hunched over in Amma's hut, tears streaming down his face. He had recently experienced a painful breakup and was struggling to find happiness and meaning in life.

Amma approached him and sat down beside him.

Westerner: Amma, I am feeling so lost and alone. I recently went through a painful breakup, and I can't seem to find any happiness or meaning in life.

Amma: Dear child, I understand that you are going through a difficult time. But please remember that love is always in the present. It is not something that we can hold, rather it is a state of being that is always within us.

Westerner: But how can I find happiness again?

Amma: Happiness, like love, is also in the present. It is not something that we can chase after or acquire. It is a state of being that arises when we are fully present in the moment. When we are able to let go of the past and not worry about the future, we can find happiness in the present moment.

Westerner: What about God and enlightenment?

Amma: God is always in the present, my child. He is not some far-off being that we have to strive to reach. Rather, he is always within us, in every moment. And as for enlightenment, it too is in the present. It is not something that we can achieve through effort or striving. Instead, it is a state of being that arises when we are fully present in the moment and connected to the Divine within us.

Westerner: But how do I let go of the past and be present in the moment?

Amma: It takes practice, my child. Through meditation and mindfulness, we can learn to quiet the mind and be fully present in the moment. We can learn to let go of the past and not worry about the future. Then we can *be* in the present moment. It is through this practice that we can find inner peace and happiness, and connect with the Divine within us.

The devotee bowed his head in gratitude.

Amma: Always remember that you are loved and supported. The Divine is always with you, son, and you are never alone. Keep practicing mindfulness and meditation, and you will find the peace and happiness you seek.

Commentary

Amma's words emphasizes the importance of living in the present moment, where love, happiness, God, and enlightenment abide.

Love in the Present

Amma says that love is in the present moment. By living in the present, we connect with the people around us and can begin to cultivate love for all.

Happiness in the Present

Amma reminds us that happiness can only be found in the present moment. By letting go of regrets about the past or worries about the future, we can find joy and fulfillment in the present, right now.

God and Enlightenment in the Present

God and enlightenment exist only in the present moment. By living in the present and cultivating spiritual awareness, we can connect with the divine and find fulfillment.

Conclusion

Amma's conversation with this young man reminds us to live in the present moment. By focusing on the present, we can find love, happiness, and connection in our lives. Her words remind us that it is by living in the present that we can connect with God and find enlightenment.

***

16. World
"In today's world, human beings are dying and human machines are being born in their place." – Amma

In this dialogue that follows, Amma speaks with a university Vice Chairperson about machines and technology.

VC: Amma, it is an honor to have you here at our university. Your teachings and wisdom are greatly appreciated by our students and faculty.

Amma: Thank you, my child. It is always a joy for me to share with young minds such as these.

VC: I wanted to ask you about a statement you made recently: 'In today's world, human beings are dying and human machines are taking birth.' What did you mean by that?

Amma: Son, what I meant is that in our modern world, we are becoming increasingly disconnected from our humanity. We are so focused on technology, productivity, and efficiency that we forget to nurture our relationships with one another and with the natural world around us.

VC: I see what you mean. But isn't technology also improving our lives in many ways?

Amma: Of course, my child. Technology has brought us many great advances and conveniences. But at the same time, we must be careful not to lose touch with what makes us truly human. We must remember to connect with one another on a deep and meaningful level, and to live in harmony with the natural world around us.

VC: That is a beautiful sentiment, Amma. How can we help our students and faculty to live more in tune with their humanity?

Amma: It starts with education, my child. We must teach our young people not just about technology and science, but also about love, compassion, and the importance of human connection. We must encourage them to look beyond themselves and to serve others with kindness and generosity. And we must always strive to live in harmony with the natural world around us, recognizing that we are all interconnected and interdependent.

VC: Thank you, Amma. Our university community is so blessed to benefit from your wisdom and guidance.

Amma: It is an honor and joy to share with all those who seek the path of love and compassion. May we all work together to create a more compassionate and harmonious world.

Commentary

In this conversation Amma draws attention to the modern world and the impact of technology on humanity. She is concerned that we are losing touch with our humanity as we become more reliant on machines.

The Rise of Technology

Amma cautions us about the rapid rise of technology in the modern world. From smartphones to artificial intelligence, we are becoming more reliant on machines, and less human with each passing day.

The Impact on Humanity

As we become more reliant on machines, we are becoming more isolated, less connected to the world around us, and less able to empathize with others.

The Need for Balance

Amma stresses that we must find a balance between technology and humanity. While technology can benefit us in many ways, we must also recognize the importance of human connection, empathy, and compassion in our lives.

Conclusion

Technology is having a profound impact on humanity, but we must integrate it into our lives in a balanced way. As we continue to rely on machines, we must also work to cultivate our own humanity and find ways to connect with the world around us. By doing so, we can create a compassionate society, where human beings are valued above machines.

***

17. Grace

"Grace comes out of nowhere. It can happen anytime, in any place." – Amma

As a group of Kozhikode devotees were eagerly waiting for Amma in the darshan hut, singing devotional bhajans, Amma entered. Her radiant smile illuminated the space, much like the rising sun. She expressed her delight and gratitude for the devotees' devotion and love for the Divine, and reassured them that the Divine had surely received it. The devotees bowed in reverence.

Amma: My dear children, it brings me great joy to see you all singing these beautiful devotional songs. Your devotion and love for the Divine is so inspiring.

Devotees: Amma, we are so grateful to be here in your presence. Your love and grace are a blessing to us all.

Amma: My dear children, it is not I who bring grace, but rather it is the Divine that showers us all with grace and love. Grace comes out of nowhere, at any time and in any place. We must simply open our hearts and minds to receive it.

Devotees: Amma, how can we cultivate an attitude of openness and receptivity to grace?

Amma: The key is to cultivate a deep and abiding faith in the Divine. Trust that the Divine is always with you, guiding you and supporting you, even in the most difficult times. Practice prayer and meditation, and offer all your actions and thoughts to the Divine. And always remember that love is the most powerful force in the universe. When we cultivate love in our hearts, we become channels for Divine grace and healing power.

Devotees: Amma, we are beyond blessed to have you in our lives!

Amma: Dear children, it is my joy and my privilege to serve you in whatever way I can. May we all continue on the path of love and devotion, and may we always remain receptive to the grace of the Divine.

Commentary
In this devotion-soaked dialogue, Amma reminds us that grace can appear unexpectedly and in any situation. May we always remain open to the possibility of grace in our lives.

The Nature of Grace
Amma teaches that grace is not dependent on our actions or circumstances. Grace can appear unexpectedly at any time, often in ways that we could not have anticipated.

Remaining Open
By letting go of our own expectations, and remaining open to the unexpected, we can create space for grace to appear.

Recognizing Grace
It is important to recognize grace when it appears in our lives. By paying attention to the unexpected events and experiences that occur, we can recognize the presence of grace and give thanks with a grateful heart.

Conclusion
Amma reminds us to remain open, as grace can appear unexpectedly at any moment. By letting go of our expectations and remaining open to the unexpected, we can create space for grace to appear. When grace does come to us, may we have eyes to see it and the hearts to be sincerely grateful for it

***

18. Enquiry

"The foundation of spirituality is not blind faith. It is enquiry; it is an intense exploration within one's own self." – Amma

Several years ago, a group of enthusiastic youngsters from Bangalore travelled to Amritapuri to seek Amma's guidance and wisdom. Eager to understand Amma's vision of spirituality, the youngsters posed several thought-provoking questions. As always, Amma's words were full of wisdom, compassion, and practical guidance that inspired the young visitors to deepen their own spiritual practice and embark on a journey of true self-discovery.

Youth 1: Amma, we are here because we want to know your vision of spirituality. What is the foundation of spirituality?

Amma: My dear children, the foundation of spirituality is not blind faith, as some may believe. It is a deep inquiry, an intense exploration within one's own self. Spirituality is about seeking the truth, and the truth can only be discovered through direct experience, through one's own efforts and practice.

Youth 2: Amma, can you tell us more about how we can explore within ourselves and seek the truth?

Amma: The key is to cultivate a sincere and pure heart, to be open to new ideas and experiences, and to be willing to question everything, including your own beliefs and assumptions. Dear children, practice meditation and self-reflection, and seek guidance from those who have walked the path before you. But ultimately, the truth can only be discovered through your own experience.

Youth 1: Amma, we have heard that you teach a path of love and service. Can you tell us more about that?

Amma: Love and service are the natural expression of a spiritual life. When we cultivate love and compassion within ourselves, we naturally want to serve others and alleviate their suffering. Service is not just an action, it is a state of being, a way of living our lives with love and compassion. Dear children, when we serve others with love, we are serving the Divine in all beings.

Youth 1: Amma, thank you so much!

Amma: Remember, dear ones, that the journey is long and sometimes difficult, but with sincerity and dedication, you will surely reach your destination. May you always walk with the light of love and compassion in your hearts.

Commentary

Amma emphasizes the importance of inquiry and exploration in spirituality. The conversation highlights the significance of questioning and exploring our own inner selves to gain a deeper understanding of spirituality.

The Foundation of Spirituality

Amma clearly states that the foundation of spirituality is inquiry and exploration. Spirituality require that we fearlessly question our beliefs, values, and assumptions.

Intense Exploration Within One's Self

On the spiritual path, we are called to explore our own inner selves. By turning inward and examining our thoughts and feelings, we can gain a deeper understanding of ourselves and our connection to the world around us.

Enquiry as a Tool for Spiritual Growth

Amma's words also highlight the importance of enquiry as a tool for spiritual growth. By questioning our own beliefs and exploring our own inner selves, we set the stage for spiritual growth.

Conclusion

Amma's words reminds us of the importance of inquiry and exploration in spirituality. The foundation of spirituality is not blind faith, but intense exploration within. By questioning our beliefs and exploring our own inner selves, we can gain a deeper understanding of spirituality and our place in the world. To be successful in this, we must cultivate a spirit of curiosity and openness in our spiritual practices.

***

19. Mind
"When we have light within, no darkness can affect us."
—Amma

A dedicated spiritual practitioner, who had been on the path for over twenty years, once came to Amma to discuss his daily discipline. His commitment to spiritual practice had led him on the path of self-discovery and transformation. Seeking guidance and inspiration from Amma, the man humbly shared his spiritual struggles and doubts, hoping to receive Amma's wisdom and insight. Despite his years of practice, he understood that the spiritual journey is a never-ending process of learning and growth, and he was eager to learn from Amma's vast spiritual knowledge and experience.

Spiritual Practitioner: Amma, I have been struggling with negative thoughts and emotions lately. It's like there's a darkness that has taken hold of me, and I don't know how to shake it off.

Amma: I understand how you feel, my son. But remember, when we have light within, no darkness can affect us. The key is to cultivate that inner light through spiritual practice, such as meditation, prayer, and selfless service.

Spiritual Practitioner: But Amma, how can I cultivate that inner light? I feel like I'm stuck in this darkness, and I don't know how to find my way out.

Amma: My child, the first step is to become aware of the negative thoughts and emotions that are clouding your mind. Once you become aware of them, you can begin to observe them without judgment or attachment. This will help you to gradually detach from them and create space for the light to enter.

Spiritual Practitioner: That makes sense, Amma. But what if I don't have the strength or the willpower to do this?

Amma: Son, you have more strength and willpower than you realize. Remember that the Divine is always with you, supporting and guiding you. Turn to the Divine in times of difficulty, and trust that you will receive the help and guidance you need. Remember that you are never alone, and that the light is always within you, waiting to be uncovered.

Commentary

While guiding this seeker, Amma emphasizes the importance of cultivating inner light to overcome darkness and the need to develop a sense of inner strength and resilience.

Cultivating Inner Light

Amma teaches that we must cultivate inner light to overcome darkness. By focusing on our own inner strength, we can withstand the challenges and difficulties that life may bring.

Overcoming Darkness

When we have light within, no darkness can affect us. By cultivating inner strength and resilience, we can overcome the negative influences and challenges that may come our way.

The Power of Inner Light

Inner light holds the power to transform our lives, even in the face of difficulties and challenges.

Conclusion

Inner light can overcome any darkness, but we must make efforts to develop inner strength and resilience. By focusing on our own inner light, the darkness dims, and a positive and fulfilling life begins to unfold.

***

20. Attitude

"Happiness depends on how you accept, understand and surrender to situations." – Amma

In a humble hut, tucked away in the peaceful countryside, a dedicated spiritual practitioner from Rishikesh had the opportunity to speak with Amma. This seeker had devoted much of his life to sadhana, spiritual practice, in the pursuit of inner peace and enlightenment. However, despite his efforts, he found himself struggling to find true happiness in his daily life. Seeking guidance and inspiration, he turned to Amma, who was known for her profound wisdom and compassion.

With an open heart, the seeker shared his struggles with Amma, hoping to receive guidance that would lead him to true happiness and peace. Amma listened patiently, and then offered solace, reminding the seeker that true happiness comes from within and depends on how one accepts, understands, and surrenders to situations. Her words brought comfort, clarity and a new sense of purpose to the seeker's heart.

Sadhak: Amma, I have been practicing sadhana for so many years, and yet I cannot find true happiness in my life. What am I doing wrong?

Amma: My child, happiness does not come from external circumstances, but rather from within. It depends on how you accept, understand and surrender to situations.

Sadhak: But how do I cultivate this kind of inner happiness?

Amma: It begins with self-reflection and daily practice. When difficult situations arise, try to accept them as they are, without judgment or resistance. Try to understand what lessons they may be offering you, and surrender to the present moment. By doing so, you can develop a deeper sense of equanimity and inner peace.

Sadhak: I understand, Amma. But what if I cannot accept or understand the situation? What if it is too difficult?

Amma: My child, even in the most challenging situations, there is always something to be learned. If you find it difficult to accept or understand a situation, try to surrender to it instead. Allow yourself to feel the emotions that arise, without trying to change them or push them away. With time and practice, you will find that you are able to cultivate a deeper sense of peace and happiness within yourself.

Sadhak: Deep gratitude to you, Amma. I will try my best to practice this.

Commentary

In this dialogue, Amma emphasizes that acceptance, understanding, and surrender lead to happiness. She stresses that it is our attitude towards situations that determine our sense of well-being.

Acceptance

To be truly happy, we must learn to accept. By accepting the situations that we find ourselves in, we can reduce stress and anxiety and find a sense of peace.

Understanding

If we want to be happy, understanding the lessons in the situations that arise in our lives is crucial. Only then will we be able find the deeper perspective necessary to find solutions to our problems.

Surrender

Amma suggests that surrender is central to happiness. By letting go of our attachment to desired outcomes, and by surrendering to the present moment, we find that peace and contentment come to us all on their own.

Conclusion

Amma reminds us how important acceptance, understanding, and surrender are. In fact, it is our attitude towards situations that determines our sense of well-being. By accepting the situations that we find ourselves in, seeking to understand them, and surrendering to the present moment, we can find a sense of peace, contentment and happiness. The power of our mindset in shaping our experiences cannot be overstated. It is crucial to develop a positive attitude.

***

21. Love
"Logic cuts and divides, Love joins and unites" — Amma

Once a pandit, Hindu scholar, approached Amma in her hut, seeking her guidance and insights on spiritual matters. As he was a learned scholar, onlookers thought the pandit might have specific questions about Hindu scriptures, rituals, or philosophy.

Surely the pandit was thinking that Amma, known for her wisdom and deep understanding of spirituality, would be sure to provide him valuable insights and guidance. The question the scholar asked surprised all who were present.

Pandit: Amma, I have always believed that logic and reason are the only true paths to enlightenment. Can you explain to me how love can lead us to spiritual realization?

Amma: My child, logic has its place, but it can only take us so far. The mind, with all its reasoning and analysis, can only cut and divide. Love, on the other hand, has the power to join and unite. It allows us to see the interconnectedness of all things, and to experience the oneness of the universe.

Pandit: But how can love be a path to enlightenment? Surely it is too subjective, too emotional to lead us to ultimate truth.

Amma: Love is not just an emotion, my child. It is the very essence of existence itself. It is what connects us all, and what gives life meaning and purpose. Without love, there can be no true understanding or realization.

Pandit: I understand what you mean, Amma. But how can we cultivate this kind of love in our lives?

Amma: It begins with an open heart and a willingness to connect with others. When we see others as extensions of ourselves, and treat them with kindness and compassion, we begin to experience the power of love in our lives. By practicing love in all our interactions, we can move beyond the limitations of the mind and connect with the deeper truths of our existence.

Pandit: Amma, thanks to you I will reset my course and try to integrate love into my practice and my life.

Commentary
In this powerful dialogue, Amma draws a contrast between logic and love. Whereas love is a unifying force, logic is limited in its ability to bring people together.

The Role of Logic
Amma defines logic as that which cuts and divides. While logic can be useful in analyzing and understanding the world around us, it can also lead to a sense of separation and division.

The Power of Love
Amma words and very life testify to the power of love to join and unite people. Love can bring diverse people together and create a sense of connection and unity that transcends all logical boundaries.

Love as a Unifying Force
Love is the great unifying force in the world. Amma says that by cultivating a sense of love and compassion towards others, we can create heaven on earth.

Conclusion
Amma's quote reminds us of the contrast between logic and love and emphasizes the importance of love as *the* unifying force. Logic is limited in its ability to bring people together. Love, however has the power to create a sense of connection and unity that transcends all boundaries. By cultivating a sense of love and compassion towards others, we can create a society in which people are joined and united by a sense of shared humanity.

***

22. Mind
"Human beings are slaves to their thoughts. The mind is a constant flow of thoughts." – Amma

During one Tuesday prasad-day, Amma expressed concern about the behavior of one of the brahmacharis living in the ashram. Tuesdays are a time of communal sharing of food and blessings, yet Amma took this time to address her brahmacharis about their spiritual practices and personal struggles.

She used this opportunity to help her brahmacharis manage the constant flow of thoughts and emotions that can disturb spiritual practice.

Brahmachari: Amma, I am constantly struggling with my thoughts. It seems like my mind never stops. I can't seem to control it.

Amma: Yes, it is true. Human beings are slaves to their thoughts. But *you* don't have to be a slave to them. You can be the master of your thoughts.

Brahmachari: How can I master my thoughts, Amma?

Amma: Through meditation and spiritual practices, you can train your mind to be still and focused. Just as you train your body through physical exercise, you can train your mind through mental exercises.

Brahmachari: But it is not easy to control the mind. It feels like a constant battle.

Amma: It is a battle, but it is a battle worth fighting. When you master your mind, you will experience peace and happiness like never before. Remember, the mind is a tool, and you are the one in control of it. Don't let your thoughts control you. Take charge and use your mind wisely.

Brahmachari: I will try, Amma. I will really try.

Amma: Keep up with your spiritual practices and don't give up. The mind may be a constant flow of thoughts, but you have the power to choose which thoughts to hold on to and which ones to let go of.

Commentary

In this exchange, Amma draws attention to the nature of the human mind and the constant flow of thoughts that can dominate our lives. She emphasizes that we can easily become slaves to our thoughts and that we must regain mastery over them by cultivating mindfulness and awareness.

The Nature of the Mind

The mind is always active, generating thoughts that can be both positive and negative, constructive and destructive.

Slavery to Thoughts

When we identify too closely with our thoughts, we can easily become slaves to them. They can start to control us, leading to stress, anxiety, and other negative emotions.

Cultivating Mindfulness

Thus, mindfulness and awareness are of vital importance in our lives. By becoming more aware of our thoughts and emotions, we begin to develop detachment and perspective.

Conclusion

The human mind is a constant flow of thoughts that can dominate us, if we are not careful. This is why it is so important to cultivate mindfulness and awareness in our lives. By becoming more aware of our thoughts and emotions, we can develop a sense of detachment and perspective, which will bring greater peace, clarity, and well-being. Amma reminds us that we all have the power to overcome our thoughts and emotions.

***

23. Humility

"Only the attitude 'I am nothing, I know nothing' will help you reach the goal." – Amma.

Two brahmacharis in Amma's Ashram were having a quarrel; each believed he was right. The matter eventually reached Amma, who called them both to meet with her. Amma reminded them of the importance of humility and urged them to focus on the spiritual goal.

Amma: What is this fighting that I am hearing about between the two of you?

Brahmachari 1: Amma, I was just telling him that I have done many important things in my life. But he was not ready to accept it and started boasting about himself.

Brahmachari 2: No Amma, it was the other way around. He started boasting first, and I just gave him a fitting reply.

Amma: Enough! Both of you stop this nonsense right now. Do you think this kind of behavior is acceptable in the ashram? You are supposed to be spiritual aspirants, and yet you are indulging in petty arguments over your ego.

Brahmachari 1: But Amma, I was just trying to make him understand that I am not a nobody.

Amma: That is where you are wrong. Only the attitude, 'I am nothing, I know nothing' will help you reach the goal. You are here to learn and grow spiritually, not to boost your ego. Remember that true greatness lies in humility, not in arrogance.

Brahmachari 2: But Amma, it's not that easy to let go of our ego.

Amma: I know it's not easy, but it's necessary if you want to progress on the spiritual path. You need to cultivate the attitude of surrender. Let go. Trust in the Divine and everything will fall into place.

Brahmachari 1: Sorry, Amma. We will try to do better.

Amma: That's all I can ask for. Remember, the path to self-realization is not an easy one, but with dedication, discipline, and the right attitude, you can reach your goal.

Commentary
The Role of Ego

Amma hones in on the ego in this conversation, pointing out that the ego creates separation from others and attachment to our own ideas and beliefs. This prevents us from advancing on the path.

The Importance of Humility

Amma also stresses the importance of humility in spiritual practice. By letting go of the ego and cultivating a sense of humility, we can become open to new experiences and ideas and progress towards the goal.

"I Am Nothing, I Know Nothing":

Adopting the attitude, "I am nothing, I know nothing" is helpful on the spiritual path. This attitude inspires us to let go of our attachment to our own beliefs and remain open to new experiences and perspectives.

Conclusion

The ego prevents spiritual growth; thus, letting go of the ego and cultivating a sense of humility is essential. The attitude that, "I am nothing, I know nothing" is an important aspect of spiritual practice, as it opens us up to new experiences and perspectives. By adopting this attitude, we can become more receptive to spiritual growth.

***

24. Mind

"Concentration stops the flow of thoughts. When thoughts stop, the restless mind ceases its activity." —Amma

Once Amma, surrounded by a group of ashram residents, fell into conversation after Devi Bhava. The moon's radiance illuminated Amma's face as the waves from the nearby sea lapped against the shore. The topic of discussion was concentration and how it can help calm the restless mind and stop the flow of thoughts.

Amma: Do you know what the biggest obstacle on the spiritual path is? It is the mind, the restless and wandering mind that is always thinking and chattering.

Ashram Resident 1: But how can we control our thoughts, Amma?

Amma: By developing concentration. When we concentrate on one thing, the mind stops its restless activity and the flow of thoughts stops. This is the first step towards controlling the mind.

Ashram Resident 2: But how can we concentrate when there are so many distractions around us?

Amma: Concentration is a skill that can be developed with practice. Start by focusing on something simple, like your breath or a mantra. When your mind wanders, gently bring it back to your point of focus. With practice, your concentration will improve and distractions will have less of an impact on you.

Ashram Resident 3: But what about when we have important decisions to make, and we need to think about all the options and possibilities.

Amma: Of course, there are times when thinking and analysis are necessary. But by developing concentration, you will be able to think more clearly and make better decisions. And even when you need to think, you can do so with a calm and focused mind, rather than a restless and distracted one. So, practice concentration, my children, and you will see how it can transform your life.

Commentary

Amma teaches that concentration is essential for calming the mind. By stopping the flow of thoughts through concentration, we can achieve inner peace and stillness.

The Flow of Thoughts

The constant flow of thoughts in our mind can dominate our lives if we are not aware. The mind is always active, forever generating positive and negative thoughts.

The Role of Concentration

Concentration is the key to stopping the flow of thoughts. By focusing our attention on a single object or idea, we can interrupt the flow of thoughts and achieve a sense of inner calm.

The Benefits of Calming the Mind

There are many benefits that come to us when the mind is made calm through concentration. By achieving a sense of inner calm and stillness, we can reduce stress and anxiety, improve our focus and productivity, and cultivate a greater sense of inner peace and fulfillment.

Conclusion

In this dialogue, Amma reminds us that concentration leads to a calm mind. It stills the constant flow of thoughts that tend to dominate our lives. With sincere, sustained practice, a sense of inner calm and stillness begin to dawn within. Concentration is the key.

***

25. Devotion
"The real purpose of life is to experience and realize divinity within." –Amma

One day, a group of sincere brahmacharis from the ashram came to Amma for advice. They were known for their deep spiritual practice and sincere devotion for Amma. As they sat before her, Amma could sense their eagerness to understand the true purpose of life. And so, she began to speak in depth on the subject, emphasizing the importance of experiencing and realizing the divinity within.

Amma: The true purpose of life is not to accumulate material possessions or to gain fame and success in the external world. These things are temporary and can never provide lasting happiness. The real purpose of life is to experience and realize the divinity within.

Brahmachari 1: Amma, how can we experience divinity within ourselves?

Amma: It starts with self-awareness. By turning your attention inward and observing your thoughts and emotions, you begin to recognize the divinity that is already present within you. But this requires concentration and focus, as the mind is constantly distracted by external stimuli.

Brahmachari 2: But Amma, how do we develop concentration and focus?

Amma: Through the practice of meditation and selfless service. Meditation helps you to calm the mind and cultivate inner stillness, while selfless service helps you to purify the heart and develop compassion towards others. Together, these practices can help you to experience the divinity within yourself and others.

Brahmachari 3: Amma, what does 'realizing divinity within ourselves' actually mean?

Amma: Realizing divinity within oneself is the ultimate goal of human life. It leads to a state of inner peace and contentment that is not dependent on external circumstances. As this state begins to awaken, we recognize the divinity in others and treat them with love and compassion. This is the essence of spirituality.

Brahmachari 4: Amma, how do we know if we are making progress on our spiritual practice?

Amma: You will know by the peace and joy that you experience within yourself. You will also notice a positive change in the way you relate to others and the world around you. But remember, spiritual practice is a lifelong journey, and progress is not always linear. It requires patience, persistence, and faith.

As the dialogue came to an end, the brahmacharis felt inspired and motivated to continue their spiritual practice with renewed vigor. They left Amma's presence with a deep sense of gratitude and reverence, knowing that she was their guide on the path towards realizing the divinity within themselves.

Commentary

Amma unequivocally asserts that realizing the divinity within ourselves is the real purpose of life. Her words affirm that we are all inherently divine, and that the purpose of life is to experience and realize this divinity.

The Divinity Within Us

Amma constantly reminds us that we are inherently divine. It is our task to realize this and experience it.

The Purpose of Life

By cultivating a sense of spiritual awareness and connecting with our inner selves, we can begin to awaken divinity within and eventually realize the purpose of human life.

The Importance of Spiritual Practice

Through spiritual practices such as meditation, prayer, and self-reflection, we learn to connect with our inner self and begin to experience our inherent divinity.

Conclusion

In this dialogue, Amma emphasizes that we are all inherently divine and urges us to connect with our inner selves and wake up to our inner divinity. In fact, this is the very purpose of life. Spiritual practices are essential if we are to reach this goal.

***

26. Mind
"In the name of competition, we should not develop feelings of hatred and revenge." – Amma

One day, a group of students from Amrita Vidyalayam, Amma's university, came to meet Amma. These boys were keen on excelling in all areas of their lives and were curious to know how to maintain a spirit of healthy competition without feeling hatred or revenge towards their peers. They had heard that Amma is very wise and were eager to learn from her. As they sat before Amma, she could sense their enthusiasm and began to share her insights on how to be competitive while maintaining a sense of oneness with others.

Amma: My dear children. I am happy to see your enthusiasm to excel in life. But we must understand that competition should never be at the cost of our inner peace and harmony. It is important to strive towards excellence, but not to the extent that we feel hatred or revenge towards our peers.

Boy 1: But Amma, how can we stay competitive without such emotions?

Amma: We can compete in a healthy and positive manner, by focusing on our own growth and progress rather than comparing ourselves with others. We can learn from our mistakes and work on improving ourselves, rather than trying to bring others down.

Boy 2: But what if someone else's success makes us feel inferior or jealous?

Amma: Jealousy and inferiority are born out of a lack of self-confidence and self-love. We must learn to appreciate our own unique talents and abilities and focus on our own journey rather than comparing ourselves with others. Instead of feeling jealous or inferior, we should be happy for the success of others and celebrate their achievements.

Boy 3: But Amma, sometimes competition can become intense and aggressive. How do we handle such situations?

Amma: In such situations, we must learn to remain calm and centered. We should never react with anger or aggression, but rather respond with love and compassion. It is important to remember that we are all interconnected and interdependent, and that competition should never come in the way of our oneness and unity.

Boy 4: Amma, being in your presence makes us want to be better people. It won't be easy, but we will strive to keep compassion, inner peace and harmony alive within, even as we strive to be the very best.

Amma: Always remember that the true purpose of competition is not to defeat others, but to better ourselves and realize our fullest potential. May you all be blessed with success and inner fulfillment.

Commentary

In this honest dialogue, Amma highlights the dangers of competition and the negative emotions that can arise from it. She emphasizes that we must avoid feelings of hatred and revenge in the pursuit of success.

The Nature of Competition

By its very nature, competition creates pressure, which can be channeled as either a positive force for growth and development or as a negative one, leading to jealousy, resentment, and hatred.

The Dangers of Hatred and Revenge

Too often, unhealthy competition leads to feeling of hatred and revenge. In the pursuit of success, we can become overwhelmed by these negative emotions, which often lead to destructive behavior and long-lasting negative consequences both for ourselves and for society.

The Importance of Positive Competition

Amma advocates positive competition that promotes growth, development, and innovation for each member of society.

Conclusion

Amma's words remind us of the dangers of competition and the negative emotions that can arise from it. It is of upmost importance that we avoid feelings of hatred and revenge in the pursuit of excellence. By cultivating a sense of healthy competition and avoiding negative emotions, we can help to unlock the hidden potential in each member of society.

***

27. Peace
"Peace of mind is the real wealth." – Amma

One day, a sadhak from Karnataka Mookambika visited Amma with a heavy heart. He had recently lost his ashram, which had been taken over by politicians. Feeling lost and defeated, he approached Amma seeking guidance on how to find peace in the midst of such turmoil. Amma, her eyes brimming with compassion, welcomed the sadhak and listened patiently to his concerns, and then loving responded.

Amma: My child, I understand how difficult it must be for you to lose your ashram. But remember, true peace lies within us and not in external circumstances. It is important to cultivate a peaceful mind regardless of the situation we find ourselves in.

Sadhak: But how can I find peace when I have lost everything that was important to me?

Amma: You have not lost everything, my child. You still have yourself, your mind, and your spirit. These are the most valuable things that you possess. Realize that peace of mind is the real wealth. It is the key to finding happiness and contentment in life.

Sadhak: But how do I attain peace of mind when I am so disturbed?

Amma: Start by accepting the situation as it is. Do not resist it or fight against it. Instead, surrender to the will of the divine and trust that everything happens for a reason. Practice mindfulness and meditation to quiet the mind and bring a sense of calmness to your being. Cultivate gratitude for what you still have and focus on the positive aspects of your life. And always remember, you are never alone. The Divine is always with you, guiding and supporting you every step of the way.

Sadhak: Thank you, Amma. I will try my best to find peace within.

Amma: May the Divine bless you and guide you on your journey towards inner peace.

Commentary

In this dialogue, Amma speaks of inner peace as the only true wealth, the ultimate goal, and the source of all happiness and well-being.

Peace of Mind

Amma defines peace of mind as the absence of mental unrest, stress, and anxiety. This state of inner calm and tranquility leads to greater focus, clarity, and well-being.

The Importance of Inner Peace

While external possessions and accomplishments can bring temporary happiness, true happiness and fulfillment come from within, through the cultivation of inner peace. Thus, inner peace is the only true wealth.

Cultivating Inner Peace

We can touch the inner peace within ourselves through practices such as meditation, mindfulness, and self-reflection. This inner calm and tranquility naturally bring a sense of happiness, and fulfillment into our lives.

Conclusion

Amma's conversation with the sadhu remind us that inner peace is the true measure of wealth. When we are at peace, mental unrest, stress, and anxiety disappear and a sense of greater well-being, happiness and fulfillment arise within us. We invite peace into our lives by the regular practice of meditation, mindfulness, and self-reflection. When we are at peace, we learn to balance the craving for external success with inner spiritual fulfillment.

***

28. Mind

"In most cases, worldly love ends in hatred and deep sorrow." — Amma

One day, a young couple came to seek Amma's guidance with heavy hearts. They had once loved each other deeply and had defied their families to marry against their wishes. However, over time, their relationship had deteriorated, and they found themselves consumed by egoistic resentment towards each other. Unable to reconcile their differences on their own, they came to Amma hoping she could help them resolve their issues and find a way to rebuild their love. Amma listened to their concerns and then spoke of the pitfalls of worldly love and how it often leads to hatred and deep sorrow.

Amma: My dear children, it's very common in this world to mistake infatuation and attachment for love. True love is selfless and unconditional. It's a divine feeling that brings two souls closer, not just physically but emotionally and spiritually. What you are both experiencing now is not love, but rather a form of attachment. Attachment is a bond that arises from our ego and desires; it's not sustainable in the long run.

Wife: But Amma, we were so in love with each other. We defied our families to be together, and now we hate each other. How can you say that it was not love in the beginning?

Amma: What you both felt was not love, but rather a strong attachment. Attachment is conditional and depends on various factors such as physical appearance, status, and material possessions. Once these conditions are no longer met, attachment can easily turn into resentment and hatred. True love is unconditional and goes beyond these external factors.

Husband: But Amma, how can we rebuild our love? Can you give us any advice?

Amma: You can start by letting go of your ego and expectations. Love is not about who's right or wrong, but rather about accepting and understanding each other. You both need to work on yourselves individually and then come together to build a foundation of trust and respect. Only then can true love blossom. Remember, peace of mind is the real wealth. And true love brings peace and harmony to our minds and hearts.

Commentary

In this conversation, Amma highlights the pitfalls of worldly love and its tendency to lead to negative emotions such as hatred and sorrow. Thus, in relationships it is important to cultivate a sense of spiritual love that transcends the limitations of worldly love.

The Nature of Worldly Love

Amma points out the limited nature of worldly love and its potential to lead to negative emotions such as jealousy, anger, and sorrow. Worldly love is often based on attachment and desire and often leads to suffering and pain.

The Importance of Spiritual Love

Amma urges us to cultivate spiritual love, which transcends the limitations of worldly love. Spiritual love is based on a profound understanding of our interconnectedness and the nature of the universe. By its very nature, spiritual love leads to fulfillment and inner peace.

The Path to Spiritual Love

The path to spiritual love involves practices such as self-reflection, compassion, and service to others. By cultivating empathy and making efforts to connect with others, spiritual love will begin to dawn within us.

Conclusion
Worldly love is limited and often leads to negative emotions such as hatred and sorrow. Whereas, spiritual love is transcendent and leads to fulfillment and inner peace. Practices such as self-reflection, compassion, and service pave the way to spiritual love, leading to greater empathy and a sense of connection with others.

***

29. Mind

"With a purified mind, we can feel the pain of others as our own." – Amma

Once, a brahmachari-doctor visited Amma and expressed his deep concern for his cancer patients. He shared how he felt the pain of these patients and wished he could alleviate it in some way. The doctor was known for his compassionate heart and had dedicated his life to serving those in need. Amma listened attentively to his words and began to share her thoughts on the power of a purified mind and how it enables one to feel the pain of others as their own. During their conversation, Amma imparted some valuable insights on the role of love and compassion in healing and how it can bring comfort and relief to those who are suffering.

Doctor: Amma, I am deeply concerned about the cancer patients I see in my work. It pains me to see them suffer so much.

Amma: Yes, son, it is natural to feel the pain of others when we have a purified mind. When we see the suffering of others, we realize how much we are all connected. It is important to cultivate compassion and love for all beings.

Doctor: But Amma, sometimes I feel helpless. I wish I could take away their pain.

Amma: Your love for your patients helps them transcend their pain when they see you. It is important to remember that love and compassion have a powerful healing effect. When we share love and kindness with others, we can help to ease their suffering, even if it is just for a moment. Keep serving with a compassionate heart, son. Your work is important, and it is making a difference in the lives of all those you help.

Commentary
The Importance of a Purified Mind

A purified mind is free from negative emotions such as anger, jealousy, and resentment; thus, it naturally empathizes with others and compassionately reaches out to alleviate their suffering.

The Role of Spiritual Practice

Spiritual practices, such as meditation, help to purify the mind and awaken compassion. It is important to remember, though, that we are meant to reach out, walk the talk, and help whenever we can.

Conclusion

Amma reminds us that a purified mind expresses itself with empathy and compassion towards others. When we begin to feel the pain of others as our own, it is a sure sign that our minds are becoming pure. Spiritual practices not only purify our minds but also lead to a sense of inner calm and stillness, a sense of connection with others and a desire to serve.

***

30. Death

"Death is part of life. All of us must face it today or tomorrow. The important thing is not how we die, but how we live." —Amma

In the midst of a funeral procession for a dear devotee who had passed away, Amma spoke about the inevitability of death and the importance of living a meaningful life. The devotee who had passed away had dedicated his life to selfless service, and Amma praised him for his tireless efforts to help others. Some of the ashram residents, who had gathered around Amma, asked her about the secret to his peaceful death.

Sitting amidst the ashram residents, Amma spoke.

Amma: Today, we are reminded of the impermanence of life. Death is a natural part of life, and all of us must face it sooner or later. It is not in our hands to decide how we die, but we can choose how we live.

Resident 1: What was the secret to his peaceful death?

Amma: He lived a life of selfless service, always putting the needs of others before his own. He did not fear death, for he knew that it was simply a transition to another plane of existence. His peaceful death reflected the peaceful life he led.

Resident 2: Amma, how can we prepare ourselves for death?

Amma: We must live our lives with love, compassion, and selflessness. We must cultivate a deep connection with the divine and surrender ourselves to it. Only then can we face death with equanimity, knowing that we have done our very best to serve humanity and to fulfill our purpose in life. Remember, death is not the end, but merely a transition to another form of existence. We can honor this son who passed away by continuing the work he did for humanity and living lives of service for others. By doing this when loved ones die, we honor their legacy and help to create a better world.

Commentary

Amma reminds us here that death is inevitable and that the death of those we love is a powerful opportunity to reflect on how we are living our own lives. Death is a natural part of life. What truly matters is how we live our lives before we die.

Understanding Death

Amma's words highlight the need to understand death as a natural part of life. By accepting the inevitability of death, we can focus on living our lives to the fullest and making the best use of our time.

The Importance of Living

Death can inspire us to cultivate a sense of purpose and meaning in our lives, leading us to greater fulfillment and happiness right here, right now.

Living with Purpose

By setting goals, cultivating relationships, and pursuing our passions, our lives become meaningful and fulfilling.

Conclusion

Amma urges us to focus on how we live our lives, rather than on how we will die. She further exhorts us to understand death as a natural part of life that can lend a greater sense of purpose and meaning. By setting goals, cultivating relationships, and pursuing our passions, we can live our lives in a way that is meaningful and fulfilling. Amma's words reminds us to live in the present moment and to make the most of our time on earth.

***

31. Awareness

"What you lack is not knowledge, but awareness. If we continuously keep our attention on self-awareness, we will be able to experience peace and happiness." – Amma

One day, a group of sadhaks from Haridwar along with some residents from the ashram approached Amma and asked her about the importance of awareness in life. They were curious to know how to cultivate self-awareness.

Amma smiled at them and began to speak.

Sadhak 1: Amma, we have been seeking knowledge for so long, but we still feel lost and unfulfilled. Can you guide us about what we are missing?

Amma: What you lack is not knowledge, but awareness. You all have enough knowledge, but you need to work on your awareness. If we continuously maintain attention on self-awareness, we will be able to experience peace and happiness.

Sadhak 2: But Amma, how do we cultivate self-awareness?

Amma: By constantly observing our thoughts and actions and being present in the moment. When we are mindful of ourselves, we become more conscious of our true nature and can tap into the peace and happiness within us.

The sadhaks and residents listened attentively as Amma continued.

Amma: Awareness is the ability to be present in the moment and observe your thoughts, emotions, and actions without judgment. It allows us to be fully present in each moment and make conscious decisions. Without awareness, we can easily get lost in our thoughts and emotions, and this can lead to stress, anxiety, and unhappiness.

If we continuously maintain attention on self-awareness, we will be able to experience peace and happiness. We will be able to see our thoughts and emotions for what they are and not get carried away by them. We will also be able to see the beauty of the world around us and appreciate the present moment.

The sadhaks and residents nodded in agreement, brimming with gratitude for the light Amma had shed on their path.

Amma: So, my dear children, make a conscious effort to be aware of your thoughts, emotions, and actions in each moment. Practice mindfulness, meditation, and self-reflection. These practices will help you cultivate the awareness you need to experience peace and happiness in your life.

The ashram residents were hungry for even more of Amma's wisdom and persisted with their questions.

Resident 1: Amma, we have been living in the ashram for so long, but we still struggle with our inner demons. Can you help us find inner peace?

Amma: Like these seekers from Haridwar, what you lack is not knowledge, but awareness. If we continuously maintain attention on self-awareness, we will be able to experience peace and happiness.

Resident 2: Amma, can you explain how we can become more self-aware in our daily lives?

Amma: It starts with being mindful of our thoughts and actions, and making a conscious effort to be present in the moment. When we become more aware of ourselves, we can start to understand our true nature and find the peace and happiness that reside within us. It's a continuous process, but with practice and dedication, we can all achieve it.

Commentary

In this exchange, Amma emphasizes the crucial role of self-awareness in achieving peace and happiness. Most of us have knowledge, but we lack awareness. By focusing more and more on self-awareness, we are sure to experience greater well-being.

The Nature of Awareness

Awareness is a state of mindfulness and attention to our inner experience and to our outward actions. Awareness involves being present in the moment and cultivating a deeper understanding of our thoughts, emotions, and actions.

The Importance of Self-Awareness

When self-awareness increases, a sense of peace and happiness naturally arise. As we cultivate self-awareness, inner peace and well-being begin to dawn within us.

Cultivating Self-Awareness

Awareness can be developed through practices such as meditation, mindfulness, and self-reflection.

Conclusion

Self-awareness opens the door to greater well-being. When we are mindful and pay attention to our inner experience, insights and inner peace come uninvited. Spiritual practices such as meditation, mindfulness, and self-reflection, along with efforts to remain in the present moment, help us to develop self-awareness.

***

32. Prayer
"Pray, 'O Lord, both in happiness and in sorrow, grant me the boon to remember You without fail.'" —Amma

Years ago, during darshan, an old lady asked Amma to help her remember God in all situations, just like Kunthi remembered Sri Krishna. The lady believed that more sorrow would help her to always remember God. Amma responded with gentleness that the old lady should not pray for suffering but instead use the power of prayer itself to remember God.

Old Lady: Amma, I want to remember God like Kunthi remembered Sri Krishna. She remembered Him in both happy and sad times.

Amma: Yes, Kunthi's devotion to Sri Krishna was unwavering. She remembered Him even during times of great difficulty.

Old Lady: I want to remember God too, but sometimes it's hard. Maybe if I had more sorrow, it would be easier to remember Him.

Amma: It is true that sometimes difficult experiences can bring us closer to God. However, we don't need to seek out suffering to remember Him. We can pray to Him in both happy and sad times.

Old Lady: How can I pray to Him all the time?

Amma: Pray with sincerity, from the depths of your heart. Ask God for the strength to remember Him in all situations, whether it's during times of joy or sorrow. Pray, 'O Lord, both in happiness and in sorrow, grant me the boon to remember You without fail.'

Old Lady: That's a beautiful prayer. I will remember it and pray to God always.

Amma: Yes, my dear child. With prayer and a sincere desire to remember God, we can experience peace and happiness in all circumstances.

Commentary

Amma emphasizes the importance of prayer as a means of staying connected to the divine in good times and bad. By praying to remember the divine without fail, we create a constant connection with Him.

The Power of Prayer

Prayer is a powerful means of staying connected to the divine in all situations. It can help us cultivate a deeper sense of connection to something greater than ourselves and provide comfort and solace in times of distress.

The Importance of Remembering the Divine

In this conversation, Amma emphasizes the importance of remembering the divine in both good times and bad. By staying connected to the divine, we experience inner peace, well-being and purpose.

Praying for Connection

Amma recommends sincerely praying for the ability to remember the divine without fail. Cultivating a constant sense of connection to the divine brings solace and strength.

Conclusion

Prayer is a powerful means of staying connected to the divine in all situations. It provides comfort and solace in times of distress. By praying for the ability to remember the divine without fail, in good time and bad, we experience constant connection with God and greater fulfillment and happiness.

***

33. Death

"Be like a bird sitting on a dry twig. The bird knows that the twig can break at any moment and is ready to take off at any time." —Amma

In a small hut nestled amidst the lush greenery of the ashram, a wise old man sat in deep thought. He had been living in the ashram for many years and had dedicated his life to the pursuit of spiritual enlightenment. However, he was plagued by a constant worry that death would snatch him away from the ashram he loved so much.

One day, he finally approached Amma with his concern.

Old Man: Amma, I am worried about what will happen when I die. I have dedicated my life to this ashram, and I don't want to leave it.

Amma: My child, death is an inevitable part of life. We cannot escape it, but we can prepare ourselves for it. What is it that worries you?

Old Man: I worry that I will have to leave the ashram, and that my spiritual journey will come to an end.

Amma: Do not worry about the future, my child. Instead, focus on the present moment. Remember the proverb, 'Be like a bird sitting on a dry twig. The bird knows that the twig can break at any moment and is ready to take off at any time.' We must live our lives in a state of readiness, always aware of the fragility of life and the inevitability of death.

Old Man: I understand, Amma. But how do I prepare myself for death?

Amma: By living a life of purpose and meaning, and by cultivating inner peace and contentment. Focus on your spiritual journey, and trust that the universe will guide you towards your ultimate destination. Remember that death is not the end, but a new beginning.

Old Man: Thank you, Amma.

Amma: You are always welcome to come to me, my child. Remember to live each moment to the fullest, and to embrace whatever comes your way with grace and acceptance.

Commentary

To illustrate the state of being prepared for change, Amma uses the metaphor of a bird sitting on a dry twig. By being flexible and adaptable, like a bird, we can navigate life's challenges with subtlety and grace.

Embracing change

Amma encourages us to embrace change and to be prepared for unexpected events. By recognizing that situations can change at any moment, we can cultivate a sense of flexibility and adaptability that can help us navigate life's challenges with greater dexterity and ease.

The importance of readiness

We must be ready to act when needed. By staying alert and prepared for change, we can avoid becoming complacent and develop self-confidence and resilience.

Finding balance

Amma's words encourage us to find balance between being prepared and being present in the moment. By cultivating awareness, we can stay focused on the present while also being prepared for the future.

Conclusion

In this conversation, Amma reminds us to be prepared for change and ready to adapt to new situations. She encourages us to be flexible and adaptable in navigating life's challenges, to find a balance between being prepared for the future and living in the present moment. By embracing change and staying alert, we can cultivate self-confidence and resilience. We must be ready for anything, and the power of mindfulness and awareness will help us to do this.

***

34. Compassion

"In times of tragedy, our duty is to lend a helping hand to those in grief and so we light lamps of kindness and compassion." – Amma

In the wake of the devastating earthquake that struck Gujarat, a state in western India, the people were left in a state of shock and grief. The earthquake had claimed countless lives, destroyed homes, schools, and hospitals, and left many people injured and homeless. In this time of tragedy, the people of Gujarat needed all the help and support they could get to cope with the aftermath.

Amma called upon a few brahmacharis to step forward and offer their services to the people of Gujarat. She instructed them to do whatever was possible to ease the suffering of the people, from providing shelter, food, and warm clothes, to arranging for hospital treatment and ambulance services for the injured.

The brahmacharis were eager to heed Amma's call, and they set out for Gujarat with a deep sense of compassion in their hearts. They worked tirelessly to attend to every detail of the villagers' needs, serving the injured, helping to clear the rubble, and providing support to those who had lost loved ones.

Through their selfless actions and unwavering dedication, the brahmacharis became a beacon of hope and light in the darkness, spreading Amma's message of kindness and compassion to those who needed it most. Amma teaches that in times of tragedy, it is our duty to come together as a community and lend a helping hand to those in grief. By doing so, we light lamps of kindness and compassion that will guide us all towards a brighter future.

The moment the brahmacharis returned to the ashram, they went directly to Amma.

Brahmachari 1: Amma, we have returned from Gujarat. It was a life-changing experience. The people were so grateful for our help, and we were able to make a difference in their lives.

Amma: I am so proud of you, my children. Your selfless service to those in need is a true reflection of the teachings of our ashram. Tell me, what did you learn from your experience?

Brahmachari 2: We learned that service is not just a duty, but a privilege. When we give of ourselves to others, we receive so much more in return. We connected with the people of Gujarat on such a deep level, and felt one with them.

Amma: Yes, my children, service is not just about giving, but also about receiving. When we serve others, we open ourselves up to receiving their love and gratitude, and we form deep and meaningful connections with them. This is the true essence of service.

Brahmachari 3: We also learned that service is not just about helping others in times of need, but it is a way of life. We should strive to be of service to others in everything we do, whether it is through our work, our relationships, or our daily interactions with people.

Amma: Yes, my child, service is not just an action, but a state of being. When we make service a way of life, we transform ourselves and those around us. We become beacons of light and hope, spreading kindness and compassion wherever we go.

Brahmachari 1: Thank you, Amma, for giving us this opportunity. We will continue to serve others with love and humility and hope to inspire others to do the same.

Amma: My children, the path of service is not an easy one, but it is the most rewarding. As you continue on your journey, remember to serve others with joy and dedication, and may your actions light the way for others to follow.

Commentary

Amma consistently responds with compassion and kindness in times of tragedy. In fact, she sees it as our duty to lend a helping hand to those in grief and to bring light into difficult situations.

Compassion in times of tragedy
By extending kindness, understanding and compassion to those who are suffering, we can help to ease their pain and bring a sense of comfort and support.

The power of helping hands
By providing practical assistance to those in grief, we can help those who are suffering to cope with their situation and find a way forward.

Bringing Light to Darkness
It is our duty to bring light to difficult situations. By showing compassion and kindness, we can bring hope and optimism to those who are struggling and help them to create a brighter future.

Conclusion
When tragedy strikes, compassion and kindness should motivate us to lend a helping hand. By extending compassion and kindness to those who are suffering, we can help to ease their pain and bring a sense of comfort and support to them. Tragedies remind us that we are a community and that we should come together and support one another in times of need.

***

35. Mind

"Don't feel bad if someone speaks ill of you. Think that this, too, is for your own good." – Amma

The villagers who lived near the ashram were known for their conservative views and their reluctance to accept new ideas. They often spoke ill of the ashram and its residents, criticizing them for their lifestyle and their beliefs. One day, a group of ashram residents were crossing the river by boat when they overheard the villagers speaking ill of them. This left them feeling hurt and disappointed. They went to Amma to seek her guidance.

Ashram Resident 1: Amma, we feel so hurt by what the villagers said about us. They spoke ill of our way of life and criticized us for everything we stand for. It's hard not to take it personally.

Amma: My child, do not let their words affect you. Remember that they are speaking from their own perspective, and their words reflect their own limitations and fears. What they say about you is not a reflection of who you are, but of who they are.

Ashram Resident 2: But Amma, it still hurts. We are only human, and it's hard not to feel bad when people speak ill of us.

Amma: I understand, my child. But you must also understand that everything that happens to you is for your best. Even if someone speaks ill of you, it is an opportunity for you to grow and learn. You can use their words as a mirror to reflect on yourself and see if there is anything you need to change or improve.

Ashram Resident 3: That's a good point, Amma. We should not take criticism personally, but use it as an opportunity for self-reflection and growth.

Amma: Exactly, my child. Do not let others' words hold you back or limit your potential. Instead, use them as a catalyst for your own growth and development. Remember, everything that happens to you is for your best, even if it doesn't feel like it at the time.

The ashram residents left Amma's presence feeling lighter and more at peace. They realized that they had the power to choose their own reactions to others' words and actions, and that every experience, good or bad, was an opportunity for growth and learning.

Commentary

Amma suggests that when we are criticized, rather than feeling bad, we can use it as an opportunity for self-reflection and self-improvement.

The Nature of Criticism

Suffering the barbs of criticism is a common experience in life. Criticism can take many forms and can come from endless sources, including friends, family, and coworkers.

The Importance of Reframing

When we receive negative criticism, it is important to reframe it and use it as an opportunity for growth and self-improvement. Rather than feeling bad about criticism, we can use it as a way to identify our weaknesses and improve.

The Power of Positive Thinking

Amma reminds us to stay positive when handling negative criticism. By reframing criticism, we learn to make lemonade out of lemons and cultivate a sense of optimism and resilience that can help us navigate life's challenges with dexterity.

Conclusion

Amma encourages us to reframe negative criticism and use it as an opportunity for growth and self-improvement. Positive thinking is the best way to handle criticism, as it helps us cultivate the qualities of optimism and resilience in the face of challenges. By using criticism as a means to identify where we can improve, we become better versions of ourselves. Self-awareness is essential in helping us to accept criticism as a precious opportunity to improve.

***

36. Relax

"Whatever you do and wherever you are, relax and you will see how much power you will gain." – Amma

The ashram brahmacharis had been working hard for weeks, taking care of various tasks and responsibilities. As a result, they had become stressed and tense, with little time for relaxation or reflection. One day, Amma noticed their strained expressions and decided to take them to the nearby beach to unwind and meditate. She encouraged them to let go of their worries and to be present in the moment.

Amma: My dear children, I can see that you are all feeling very tense and stressed. You have been working hard and have had little time for relaxation. That is why I have brought you here to the beach, to help you relax and rejuvenate.

Brahmachari 1: Thank you, Amma. We really need this break. We have been working so hard that we feel like we are at our wit's end.

Amma: I understand, my child. But remember, relaxation is not just a physical activity, it is also a state of mind. When you are relaxed, you become more open to the world around you, and you gain a greater sense of power and control.

Brahmachari 2: But how do we relax, Amma? We feel like we are always on the go, with little time to slow down.

Amma: Relaxation is not about doing anything special. It is about being present in the moment and letting go of your worries and fears. Look at the waves, the sun, the birds. Feel the sand between your toes. Breathe deeply and let go of your thoughts.

The brahmacharis spent some time sitting on the beach, watching the waves and feeling the warm sun on their skin. Then, Amma led them in a meditation, helping them to focus on their breath and let go of their thoughts.

After the meditation, Amma took time to talk with each of the brahmacharis about their worries and concerns. Amma listened with compassion and offered insights and individual guidance, helping each one of them to see their problems in a new light.

As they left the beach, the brahmacharis felt more relaxed and at peace. They realized that relaxation was not just a luxury, but a necessity for their well-being. They were grateful to Amma for reminding them to relax and recharge.

Commentary

Amma emphasizes the importance of relaxation and its positive impact on our well-being. In fact, by relaxing, we gain a greater sense of power and control in our lives.

The Importance of Relaxation

Amma encourages us to relax so that we can enjoy a state of calm and well-being. By relaxing, we can reduce stress and anxiety and improve our overall sense of health and happiness.

The Power of Relaxation

Relaxation also brings a greater sense of control and confidence in our lives. By taking time to relax, we can recharge our energy and approach life's challenges with a renewed sense of vigor and purpose.

Relaxation Techniques

Amma encourages us to experiment and find relaxation techniques that work for us. Whether it's practicing meditation, taking a nature walk, or engaging in a favorite hobby, finding ways to relax can have a profound impact on our overall sense of well-being.

Conclusion

Relaxation promotes a sense of calm and well-being, confidence and control in our lives. By finding relaxation techniques that work for us, we can improve our overall sense of health and happiness and approach life's challenges with greater ease and resilience.

***

37. Japa
"If you are unable to meditate, chant your mantra or sing bhajans." —Amma.

One of Amma's devotees was in the ashram hospital recovering from an illness. One day, as she was resting in her bed, Amma came to check on her. During the visit, Amma asked her if she was chanting her mantra.

Amma: My child, how are you feeling today?

Devotee: I'm doing better, Amma. Thank you so much for coming to visit.

Amma: I'm happy to hear you are doing better. Have you been chanting your mantra japa in the hospital?

Devotee: No, Amma. I haven't been able to focus on my practice since I've been here.

Amma: I see. Well, chanting mantras and singing bhajans is a helpful alternative when you are unable to meditate. Would you like me to show you how?

Devotee: Yes, Amma. I would love that.

Amma then sat next to the devotee and began to sing a bhajan. The devotee joined in, feeling the vibrations of the music and the power of the words. Amma encouraged her to continue chanting and explained the benefits of mantra japa and bhajans.

Amma: Chanting mantras and singing bhajans are powerful tools for focusing the mind and connecting with the divine. They purify the mind and calm the emotions. Even if you are unable to meditate, these practices can still bring peace and clarity.

Devotee: Amma. I feel much better now.

Amma: I am glad, my child. Remember, even if you are facing challenges or difficulties, there is always a way to connect with the divine. Through chanting, singing, or meditation, you can always find a way to connect with the source of all peace and happiness.

Commentary
Amma offers practical advice for those struggling with meditation. If we are unable to meditate, there are other spiritual practices we can do to connect with the divine.

The Challenge of Meditation
Amma understands that meditation can be a challenge for some of her children. While meditation is a powerful tool for spiritual growth and well-being, it can also be difficult for some to practice.

Alternative Spiritual Practices
Consequently, Amma offers alternative spiritual practices that work for everyone. Whether it's chanting a mantra or singing bhajans, there are many different ways to cultivate a sense of inner peace and connection with the Divine.

The Importance of Persistence
Persistence is essential in our spiritual practices. Even if we struggle with meditation, we can continue to explore different techniques until we find what works best for us.

Conclusion
This conversation reminds us to use alternative spiritual practices if we are struggling with meditation. By persisting in our spiritual practice, and exploring different techniques, we invite the peace of the divine into our lives. Self-awareness is vital in helping us stay open to new spiritual practices.

***

38. Master
"Try to imbibe the Master's teachings and make them part of your life." – Amma

Ram was feeling disturbed while doing seva in the cowshed. Amma noticed his distress and went over to talk to him. Ram expressed how difficult it was to integrate Amma's teachings into his daily life. Amma sat with him among the cows and began a conversation about the importance of *living* the Master's teachings.

Amma: Ram, my child, how are you doing?

Ram: I'm feeling a little disturbed, Amma. I'm not sure how to incorporate your teachings into my life.

Amma: I understand. It can be challenging to apply spiritual principles into our day-to-day lives. But it's important to try. Remember, the Master's teachings are not just words. They are a way of living.

Ram: Yes, Amma. But how can I make them a part of my life?

Amma: One way is to practice mindfulness. Be aware of your thoughts, words, and actions. Ask yourself, 'Is this in line with the Master's teachings'?

Ram: That's such good advice, Amma. But what about when I forget?

Amma: Don't worry about forgetting. It's natural. Just keep practicing. And when you do forget, use it as an opportunity to learn and grow. Reflect on what happened and how you can do better next time.

Ram: Amma, I'm so grateful for your guidance.

Amma: Remember, my child, the Master's teachings are not just for studying. They are for living. Try to imbibe them and make them a part of your life. When you do, you will see how much they can transform you.

Commentary

Amma urges us to incorporate the teachings of our spiritual master into our daily life. When we imbibe the wisdom of our master, well-being and fulfillment are sure to follow.

The Importance of Spiritual Teaching

Spiritual teachings are pivotal in promoting personal growth and development. They are essential guides that show us how to live and act in the world.

Imbibing the Teachings

The teachings of spiritual masters must be taken to heart and made a part of our day-to-day lives. We must embody the wisdom of spiritual masters, not just talk about it.

The Significance of Integration

By living in accordance with the wisdom of spiritual masters, we can align our actions with our values and revive a sense of purpose in our lives.

Conclusion

Amma is clear that the teachings of spiritual masters must be integrated into our daily lives, if they are to have transformative power. Spiritual teachings are meant to spark personal growth and development; thus, the wisdom of spiritual masters must be imbibed into our being and integrated into our actions. A spiritual teacher's guidance is imbued with power. If we stay open to their wisdom, we will surely move forward on the path.

***

39. Present Moment

"An action always takes place in the present moment. In order to function fully, to be complete and perfect in your actions, you have to learn to live in the present moment."

– Amma

As Amma was doing construction seva, she noticed one of the bramacharis had become distracted by a fight between a bird and a cat. Amma called him over to remind him of the importance of living in the present moment.

Amma: My child, what are you looking at?

Bramachari: Oh, Amma. I was just watching a bird and a cat fight.

Amma: I see. But remember, in order to function fully and be complete in your actions, you have to learn to live in the present moment.

Brahmachari: Yes, Amma. But it's not always easy to stay focused.

Amma: I understand. The mind can be easily distracted. But with practice, you can learn to control it. When you find yourself getting distracted, try to bring your attention back to the present moment. Focus on your breath, the task at hand, or the people around you.

Brahmachari: Okay, Amma. I will try to be more mindful.

Amma: Good! When you live in the present moment, you can perform your actions fully and completely. You become more efficient, more effective, and more fulfilled in everything you do. Son, always strive to live in the present moment.

Commentary

Here Amma emphasizes the importance being present and fully focused in our actions. When we are focused in the present moment, our actions become efficient and effective.

The Significance of the Present Moment

Being awake in the present moment brings a sense of aliveness into our actions and experiences. We begin to feel relaxed, focused and content while acting in the world.

The Importance of Full Engagement

Amma encourages us to be present and focused in the present moment while performing our actions. If we can do so, we will find that the quality and effectiveness of our actions exponentially improves.

The Role of Mindfulness

Mindfulness is the gateway to present-moment awareness. By practicing mindfulness and staying present in the moment, we can improve our overall sense of well-being and become more effective in our actions.

Conclusion

In order to complete our actions properly, we must be in the present moment. By cultivating present-moment awareness through mindfulness, we can improve the quality of our actions and enjoy greater success and peace.

***

40. Love

"Unconditional love and compassion are expansiveness, like the sky." –Amma

During a darshan-line seva, a man was shouting at a devotee who was trying to cut the line. Another person who was overseeing the line came running and pulled the devotee back into his proper place in line. Amma, who had seen the whole incident, called the two men over to remind them about the importance of unconditional love and compassion.

Amma: My dear children, what happened here?

Darshan sevite: Amma, this man was trying to jump the line, so I had to shout at him to maintain order.

Devotee: Amma, I didn't mean to jump the line. I was just trying to get a closer look at you.

Amma listened to the man, then directed her attention to the sevites.

Amma: My sons please remember, no matter what the situation is, we must always approach it with unconditional love and compassion. When we treat others with kindness, we create expansiveness in our hearts, like the sky.

Darshan sevite: But Amma, sometimes people can be very difficult to deal with.

Amma: I understand. But when we respond with anger and aggression, we only create more negativity. Instead, try to approach every situation with an open heart and a peaceful mind. Remember that everyone is fighting their own battles, and we must do our best to support them with love and compassion.

Darshan Sevite: Sorry Amma. I promise I will try to do better.

Amma: Good, my child. When we approach life with love and compassion, we create a positive ripple effect that touches everyone around us. So always remember to lead with your heart and to treat others with kindness.

Commentary
Unconditional love and compassion are expansive like the sky. They hold the power to transcend all boundaries and limitations.

The Power of Unconditional Love
Unconditional love is a transformative power. When we express it in our words and actions, barriers collapse, and we find ourselves connecting with others in a meaningful, authentic way.

The Expansiveness of Compassion
The expansiveness of compassion transforms both the giver and receiver of that compassion.

The Metaphor of the Sky
In this conversation, Amma points to the sky to illustrate the vast and all-encompassing nature of love and compassion. Just as the sky is limitless and expansive, so are love and compassion. Inspired by them, we can overcome any boundary.

Conclusion
Unconditional love and compassion are transformative. Their expansive nature inspires us to share sky-like love and compassion with all beings.

***

41. Mind

"Fewer thoughts mean more peace. More thoughts mean less peace and more agitation." – Amma

As a meditation session with Amma was drawing to a close, one of the brahmacharis asked her what to do with the many thoughts that arise during meditation. Amma took the opportunity to explain the relationship between thoughts and inner peace.

Brahmachari: Amma, I am having trouble quieting my mind. I feel like I have too many thoughts, and it's making it hard to meditate. What should I do?

Amma: My dear child, having many thoughts is natural, especially when we are trying to quiet the mind. But remember, the more thoughts we have, the more agitation we experience, and the less peace we feel.

Brahmachari: But how can I reduce the number of thoughts?

Amma: The best way is to focus on the present moment. Try to observe your thoughts without judgment, and then let them go. Focus on your breath, or a mantra, and allow your mind to settle into a state of stillness. Fewer thoughts bring more peace.

The brahmanchari folded his hands in gratitude.

Amma: Remember that meditation is a journey. It takes time and practice to quiet the mind. But with patience and perseverance, you will find the peace you seek.

Commentary

In this conversation, Amma unequivocally draws a correlation between the number of thoughts we have and the depth of our inner peace.

The Relationship Between Thoughts and Peace

Amma encourages us to reduce the number of thoughts. By minimizing mental chatter, calm and well-being become our constant companions.

The Role of Mindfulness

Mindfulness plays a central role in reducing the number of thoughts, which promotes inner peace. By practicing mindfulness, and staying present in the moment, we reduce mental agitation and develop inner stillness.

The Benefits of Peaceful Mind

The benefits of a peaceful mind include greater clarity, focus, and overall well-being. By cultivating a calm and focused mind, we can improve our ability to deal with challenges and achieve our goals with ease and grace.

Conclusion

Amma reminds us to cultivate a calm and focused mind in order to experience greater peace and well-being. By reducing the number of thoughts, we experience increased levels of inner peace, stillness, clarity, focus, and success.

***

42. Mind

"The mind is a very effective tool. We can use it to create both hell and heaven." – Amma

A doctor from Bangalore came to Amma to ask about the mind's true nature. Amma took the opportunity to explain the power of the mind and how it can be used to create either positive or negative experiences.

Doctor: Amma, can you explain what the mind is and how we can use it effectively?

Amma: My child, the mind is a very powerful tool given to us by God. It can be used to create either heaven and hell, depending on how we choose to use it.

Doctor: How can we use it to create heaven?

Amma: By cultivating positive thoughts, we can create a sense of inner peace and joy. We can use our minds to focus on the good things in our lives and to appreciate the beauty around us. We can also use our minds to cultivate compassion and kindness towards others.

Doctor: And how can we use it to create hell?

Amma: By dwelling on negative thoughts and emotions, we can create a sense of suffering and despair. When we focus on our fears and worries, our minds become clouded, and we lose touch with our true nature. We can also use our minds to harm others through negative thoughts and actions.

The doctor was speechless.

Amma: Remember, my child, the mind is like a garden. Just as you can cultivate beautiful flowers, positive thoughts, you can also let weeds, negative thoughts, take root. The choice is up to us. When we focus on negative thoughts, we create our own personal hell, but when we cultivate positive thoughts. we create our own heaven. It takes practice and discipline to train the mind to think positively, but with patience and practice, meditation, and other spiritual practices, we can succeed.

Commentary

Amma clearly states that it is the mind that shapes our experience of the world. Thus, it is crucial that we harness the power of the mind towards positive thoughts and goals.

The Power of the Mind

Amma reminds us here that the quality of our thinking plays a powerful role in determining the quality of our experiences.

The Role of Positive Thinking

By cultivating a positive and optimistic outlook, we improve our overall sense of well-being.

The Importance of Mindfulness

Mindfulness is essential if we hope to harness the power of the mind. Staying present in the moment improves our ability to manage our thoughts and emotions, which helps us to generate positive experiences in our lives.

Conclusion

Amma reminds us of the power of the mind and its role in shaping our experiences. Positive thinking and mindfulness are essential to create positive and fulfilling experiences. By harnessing the power of our thoughts and emotions, we can create a life filled with happiness, meaning, and purpose. Cultivating self-awareness and an optimistic outlook are essential if we wish to be truly happy.

***

43. Anger

"Anger is a weakness; jealousy is a weakness; hatred, selfishness and fear are all weaknesses. The root cause of all of these is the ego. Ego makes you think you are superior and others are inferior. But in the eyes of God, everyone is equal. We all have our own duties and responsibilities, and we should perform them with love and compassion towards ourselves and others. Instead of being angry or jealous, try to understand each other's point of view and find a solution that benefits everyone. Remember, the ultimate goal of life is to overcome the ego and realize our true nature, which is pure love and compassion." – Amma

One day as Amma was walking across the ashram, she came across two people arguing.

Amma: What's going on here?

Brahmachari: Amma, this householder is not doing his duties properly. He is not cleaning the vessels to prepare for the homa.

Householder: Amma, I am doing everything that is expected of me. It's the brahmachari who is not doing his part.

Amma: Is this how either of you should be behaving? Shouting and blaming each other?

Brahmachari: Amma, I am doing my duties. I don't know why he is falsely accusing me.

Householder: Amma, I am not falsely accusing him. He is not doing his work, and it's affecting the homa preparations.

Amma: (*calmly*) Both of you are getting angry and blaming each other. Do you think that's the right way to resolve this?

Brahmachari: No, Amma.

Householder: Sorry, Amma. I should not have raised my voice.

Amma: (*smiling*) It's okay. Anger, jealousy, and hatred are all weaknesses that arise from the ego. You must learn to let go of your egos and work together harmoniously.

The brahmachari and householder both nodded in agreement. Amma continued.

Amma: Instead of blaming each other, why don't you both work together to complete this homa successfully?

The brahmachari and householder both smiled broadly and replied in unison.

Brahmachari and Householder: Yes, Amma.

Amma: (*smiling back at them*) Good. Remember, it's only when we let go of our weaknesses that we can truly grow and evolve.

Commentary

This dialogue shows the negative effects of ego-based emotions such as anger, jealousy, and fear. If we wish to cultivate more positive and constructive emotions, we must transcend the ego.

The Negative Effects of Ego-Based Emotions

Emotions such as anger, jealousy, and fear bring only negative effects. These emotions inevitably create conflict and tension in our relationships, leading to a sense of inner turmoil and distress.

The Role of Ego

Ego drives the expression of negative emotions. By identifying and transcending the ego, we can reduce the impact of these emotions and cultivate more positive and constructive emotions.

The Importance of Self-Awareness

Amma's words underscore the importance of self-awareness in recognizing and managing ego-based emotions. By striving to better understand ourselves and our emotional triggers, we can reduce the impact of negative emotions and cultivate more positive outcomes.

Conclusion

Amma's words of wisdom remind us of the negative effects of ego-based emotions such as anger, jealousy, and fear. Recognizing and transcending the ego, in order to cultivate more positive and constructive emotion, is key to happiness. By practicing self-awareness and mindfulness, we can reduce the impact of negative emotions and create light out of darkness. Letting go of negative, ego-driven emotions clears the way for us to cultivate positive relationships.

***

44. Life

"Every failure is a lesson for us to learn from." – Amma

Once, a spiritual seeker from Gangotri approached an ashramite with a problem. The seeker shared that he had been unable to continue his spiritual practice due to ill health, which led him to feel lost and defeated. The ashramite suggested that he seek guidance from Amma. The seeker wisely agreed to follow his advice.

Spiritual seeker: Amma, I have failed in my spiritual practice due to ill health, and now I feel lost. What should I do?

Amma: Every failure is a lesson for us to learn from. It is important to accept and learn from our mistakes, rather than dwelling on them or feeling lost. Ill health may have hindered your spiritual practice, but it does not mean you have failed. Use this experience as an opportunity to reflect on your journey, and make necessary adjustments to your approach. Remember, the path of spirituality is not always easy, but it is worth persevering through challenges. Keep moving forward with a positive attitude and trust that the universe will guide you towards the right path.

The seeker was mesmerized. Amma continued.

Amma: Remember that setbacks are part of any journey, including the spiritual one. When we face challenges, it is easy to lose sight of our goals and feel discouraged. But it is precisely at these times that we need to practice resilience and cultivate a positive mindset. Sometimes, it is not enough to have only good intentions and effort. We need to also make sure that our approach is balanced, and we are taking care of ourselves physically, mentally, and emotionally. Remember to take care of yourself and be kind to yourself. This will not only help you in your spiritual practice but also in all aspects of life.

Seeker: But how do I ensure that my approach to the spiritual journey is correct, and how can I ensure I don't get sidetracked or lose my way?

Amma: The spiritual journey is a personal one, and it is up to each individual to find their own way. However, there are some general principles that can guide us. First, it is important to have a clear sense of purpose and intention. Why do you want to pursue spirituality? What do you hope to gain from it? When we have a clear sense of purpose, we are less likely to get sidetracked or lose focus. Second, it is important to have a regular practice, whether it is meditation, prayer, or some other form of spiritual discipline. This practice should be done with sincerity and devotion, and should be integrated into our daily lives. Finally, it is important to have the guidance of a qualified teacher or mentor, someone who has walked the path before us, who can help us navigate the challenges that arise along the way.

The spiritual seeker left the ashram feeling inspired to continue on his spiritual journey with purpose and discipline.

Commentary

Amma highlights the importance of viewing failure as a learning opportunity. We must learn to embrace failure as a natural part of the learning process and use it to improve and grow.

The Importance of a Growth Mindset

Amma suggest we develop a growth mindset, so we can view failure as a learning opportunity. By adopting a positive and optimistic outlook, we can view failure as a stepping stone to success rather than as a roadblock.

The Value of Learning

There is great value in learning to grow from failure. By reflecting on our failures and identifying areas for improvement, we can gain knowledge and cultivate new skills that can help us succeed in the future.

Overcoming Fear of Failure

It is important to overcome the fear of failure if we hope to embrace new challenges and opportunities. By recognizing that failure is a natural part of the learning process, we can reduce our fear of failure and embrace new challenges with confidence and resilience.

Conclusion

Amma reminds us to embrace failure as a learning opportunity and to cultivate a growth mindset, viewing failure as a stepping stone to success. By reflecting on our failures and identifying areas for improvement, we can cultivate new skills and knowledge that can help us succeed in the future. By overcoming the fear of failure and embracing new challenges, we connect with the confidence and resilience within us.

***

45. Nature

"Each and every object in Nature teaches us something. Renunciation and selflessness are the greatest lessons Nature teaches us ." – Amma

One day, a brahmachari in the ashram plucked a leaf from a healthy, beautiful plant. Feeling guilty, he went to Amma to confess his actions and seek guidance.

Amma: Each and every object in nature teaches us something. Renunciation and selflessness are the greatest lessons to learn from nature. The plant that you plucked was a part of nature's beauty, and by taking it away, you have disrupted its natural cycle. This may seem like a small act, but it is an important reminder that our actions have consequences, not just for ourselves, but for the world around us.

It is important to remember that nature is not ours to use however we wish, but rather something to be respected and cherished. We must learn to live in harmony with nature and strive towards a more sustainable way of living. This means making sacrifices and letting go of our attachments to material possessions, so that we can develop empathy and compassion towards all living beings.

So, my dear child, let this be a lesson to you. Let us all strive to cultivate a deeper sense of selflessness and renunciation in our lives and learn from the wisdom of nature.

As the brahmachari listened to Amma's words, he felt a sense of shame for his actions.

Brahmachari: But how can I practice selflessness and renunciation in my daily life? It seems like such a difficult thing to do.

Amma smiled gently.

Amma: It is true that renunciation and selflessness are not easy to practice, but they are essential if we want to grow spiritually. One way to practice selflessness is to cultivate a sense of empathy and compassion towards others. This means putting the needs of others before our own, and doing what we can to help those in need.

Renunciation, on the other hand, means letting go of our attachment to material possessions and desires. This does not mean that we should reject the world and live as ascetics, but that we should be mindful of our desires and not allow them to control us.

We can also learn from nature itself. Look at the trees, for example. They give us shade, oxygen, and beauty without asking for anything in return. They do not hold onto their leaves or fruits, but let them go when the time comes. If we are alert, we can learn from their example and practice selflessness and renunciation in our own lives.

The brahmachari listened intently to Amma's words, but still had questions.

Brahmachari: What about our personal goals and desires? Don't they matter?

Amma: Of course, personal goals and desires are important, but we must learn to balance them with the needs of others and the world around us. We can pursue our goals and dreams, but we must do so with a sense of responsibility and awareness of the impact of our actions on others. We must learn to live in harmony with the world, rather than at the expense of it.

The brahmachari nodded.

Brahmachari: But how can we develop empathy and compassion towards others?

Amma: (*smiling*) Empathy and compassion can only be developed through practice. We can start by simply listening to others and trying to understand their perspective. We can also perform acts of kindness and service, even if they are small. By doing such things, we begin to cultivate a sense of empathy and compassion in our hearts.

The brahmachari felt grateful for Amma's guidance and thanked her for her wisdom. He left feeling inspired and motivated to practice selflessness and renunciation in his life. He made an inner resolve to improve and to learn from the wisdom of nature.

Commentary

In this dialogue, Amma reminds us to constantly learn from nature and to imbibe the lessons it has to teach us. She also encourages us to embrace renunciation and selflessness, which we see at work in every aspect of nature.

Nature as a Teacher

We must begin to view nature as our teacher and learn from its example. By observing and appreciating the natural world, we can gain a deeper understanding of ourselves and our place in the world.

The Lessons of Renunciation and Selflessness

When we observe nature carefully, we will see renunciation and selflessness at work at every turn. If we can let go of our attachments, develop selflessness, and shift our focus to others' needs, our lives will begin to blossom.

Applying Lessons from Nature

Amma urges us to draw lessons from nature and to apply them in our daily lives. By embodying the noble qualities of nature, we can transform ourselves and the patch of the world we find ourselves in.

Conclusion

Amma's conversation with the brahmachari reminds us to learn from nature and to integrate the lessons it teaches us into our lives. Amma specifically highlights the qualities of renunciation and selflessness exemplified by Mother Nature. By observing and appreciating the natural world, we gain a deeper understanding of ourselves and our place on this Earth. By applying and integrating Mother Nature's lessons, we uplift both ourselves and the world around us.

***

46. Society

"Today's society overemphasizes skill and has relegated man to the status of mere machines." – Amma

As a spiritual leader, Amma has met and interacted with people from all walks of life. Entrepreneurs, who are often laser-focused on material success and financial gain, are no exception. In one of her interactions with an entrepreneur, Amma provided a unique perspective on the relationship between material success and inner growth.

Entrepreneur: Amma, I am working hard to grow my business and become financially successful. But sometimes I wonder if this pursuit is in conflict with my spiritual growth. Can material success and spiritual growth coexist?

Amma: Son, material success is not in conflict with spiritual growth. The conflict arises when material success becomes the sole focus of our lives, at the expense of our inner growth and the well-being of others. It is important to remember that material success is just one aspect of life. It can bring comfort and security, but it cannot provide lasting happiness and fulfillment.

The pursuit of material success should be balanced with a focus on inner growth, compassion, and service to others. When we use our success as a means to serve others and to make a positive impact in the world, it can be a source of great joy and fulfillment.

The entrepreneur nodded thoughtfully.

Entrepreneur: But how can I do this? How can I balance my pursuit of success with a focus on inner growth and service to others?

Amma: It starts with a shift in perspective. Instead of viewing success as an end in itself, view it as a means to serve others and to make a positive impact in the world. Cultivate a sense of compassion and empathy towards others, and use your success to help those in need. This will bring a sense of purpose and meaning to your work and help you find balance between material success and inner growth.

Entrepreneur: Amma, I agree with you. Society places too much emphasis on skill and too little emphasis on compassion. As an entrepreneur, I often see my employees as tools to help me achieve my business goals. How can I shift my perspective and learn to treat them as individuals?

Amma: It starts with recognizing that every person is a unique individual with their own strengths and weaknesses. When you view your employees as mere tools or resources to be used, you overlook their humanity and their potential to contribute in their own unique way. Instead, try to see them as individuals with their own passions and interests. Encourage them to bring their unique perspectives and skills to the table, and create a work environment that values collaboration and creativity.

Entrepreneur: That makes sense, Amma. But how can I balance this approach with the need to achieve business goals and stay competitive in the market?

Amma: The key is to strike a balance between achieving business goals and treating employees as unique individuals. When you create an environment that values collaboration and creativity, you can actually tap into the full potential of your employees and achieve greater success than you could have on your own. In the long run, this approach will help you build a loyal, committed team that is dedicated to achieving your business goals.

Entrepreneur: (*smiling from ear to ear*) That's a great point, Amma. But what about the larger societal pressures that encourage us to prioritize skill and efficiency over human connection and compassion?

Amma: It's true that society often values efficiency and productivity over human connection and compassion. But as individuals, we have the power to create change. We can choose to prioritize human connection and compassion in our personal and professional lives and inspire others to do the same. When we lead by example, we can create a ripple effect that has the power to transform society as a whole.

Entrepreneur: Amma, I'm so grateful I had this opportunity to be with You. You have given me a lot to think about and to strive towards in my work and personal life.

Commentary

Amma expresses concern about society's over-emphasis on skill and productivity. She advocates valuing human beings and nurturing their holistic well-being.

The Dehumanization of Society

Amma underscores the dehumanizing impact that results when societies focus exclusively on skill and productivity. By reducing human beings to mere machines, we devalue human dignity and undercut well-being.

The Importance of Holistic Well-Being

Instead, we must learn to value the entire human beings, which encompasses physical, emotional, and spiritual health. By recognizing well-being as well as productivity, we can create a more humane society.

The Need for Balance

For society to flourish, we must learn greater balance between skill and productivity on one hand and holistic well-being on the other. We are absolutely capable of doing both at the same time.

Conclusion

Amma's words reminds us of the negative impact of society's over-emphasis on skill and productivity. We must remember to value human beings as more than mere machines. By embracing a more balanced and humanistic approach, we can create a much happier world.

***

47. Self

"When you fully understand the Supreme Self, the mind won't attach itself to anything external." – Amma

Amma sat in the Kali temple on the west side, gazing at the beautiful full moon in the sky. As residents of the ashram approached her with their questions, Amma's words turned to the nature of the Self and the mind.

Ashram Resident 1: Amma, I struggle with attachment to material possessions and external things. How can I detach myself from these things and fully understand the Supreme Self?

Amma: Daughter, the key is to cultivate awareness and mindfulness in your daily life. When you are mindful, you can observe your thoughts and emotions without getting caught up in them. You can also begin to recognize the impermanence and transience of material possessions and external things. In this way, you can begin to realize that true happiness comes from within.

Ashram Resident 2: But how do we fully understand the Supreme Self? What does that even mean?

Amma: Understanding the Supreme Self means realizing your true nature as pure consciousness, pure awareness. It means recognizing that your true essence is not tied to your body, mind, or external circumstances but is eternal and unchanging. This understanding can only come through spiritual practices, such as meditation, self-inquiry, and service to others.

Ashram Resident 3: But Amma, I find it difficult to stay focused on spiritual practice when there are so many distractions in the world. How can I stay committed to this path?

Amma: It's natural to experience distractions and obstacles on the spiritual path. The key is to stay committed to your practice and to cultivate inner discipline and determination. Set aside time each day for spiritual practice, and create a supportive environment that helps you stay focused and motivated. Remember that the goal of spiritual practice is not to escape from the world, but to transform your inner state of consciousness so that you can live in the world with greater peace, joy, and compassion.

All prostrated to Amma, cherishing the wisdom she had shared with them.

Commentary

In order to understand the Supreme Self, we must overcome attachment to external things and turn our gaze inwards through spiritual practices.

The Role of Understanding

Ultimately it is understanding of the Supreme Self that will help us overcome our attachment to external things. By gaining a deeper understanding of ourselves and our place in the world, we can know true inner peace and contentment.

Overcoming Attachment

Amma urges us to reduce our attachment to external things. By recognizing that true contentment comes from within, rather than from external sources, we can reduce our attachment to material possessions and cultivate a more inwardly focused approach to life.

The Importance of Inner Realization

Inner realization is the key to developing fulfilling lives. By realizing the Supreme Self within, we can cultivate a deep inner peace that is not dependent on external circumstances.

Conclusion

Amma's dialogue with the ashram residents reminds us that we must look within to the Supreme Self to overcome attachment to external things. By recognizing that true contentment comes from within, rather than from external sources, we can cultivate a more inwardly focused, peaceful and contented life.

Amma talks with Devotees

***

48. Mind

"The more still our mind, the more it begins to resemble the universal mind." – Amma

There is a young brahmachari in Amma's ashram who dedicates his time to serving the cows and distributing the ashram's spiritual magazine, Matruvani, in the evenings. He rises early each day to perform his sadhana and then spends his mornings and afternoons tending to the cows, feeding them, and cleaning their shelter. In the evenings, he walks around the ashram grounds to distribute Matruvanis to visitors and residents, sharing the teachings and inspiration of Amma with all who are open to receive it. His devotion and service have earned him the respect and admiration of his fellow ashramites, and his humble spirit and gentle nature reflect the love and compassion that Amma inspires in her disciples.

One afternoon, as Amma sat on the veranda of the Kalari, the young brahmachari approached her and humbly asked for permission to ask a few questions. Amma graciously agreed, and the brahmachari began to share his doubts and concerns about the nature of the mind and its relationship to the universal consciousness. Despite his simple and unassuming manner, it was clear that the brahmachari had a deep and earnest thirst for spiritual knowledge, and Amma listened attentively to his each and every word with the compassionate gaze that has touched the hearts of millions.

Brahmachari: Amma, I often struggle with calming my mind during meditation. How can I still my mind and achieve a deeper level of consciousness?

Amma: Son, the key is to cultivate mindfulness and awareness in your daily life. As you become more present and attentive in your thoughts and actions, you can begin to observe the activity of your mind without getting caught up in it. This practice will naturally lead to greater stillness and clarity of mind.

Brahmachari: But what is the benefit of stilling the mind? Why is it important?

Amma: The more still our mind becomes, the more it begins to resemble the universal mind, or cosmic consciousness. This state of awareness allows us to tap into a higher level of intelligence and creativity and to experience a deeper sense of peace and harmony. It also helps us to cultivate greater compassion and empathy towards others, as we recognize our interconnectedness with all beings more and more deeply.

Brahmachari: That makes sense, Amma, but sometimes my mind feels so restless and scattered that it's hard to even begin the process of stilling it. What can I do in those moments?

Amma: When your mind feels particularly restless, it can be helpful to engage in physical practices, such as yoga or pranayama, to help release excess energy and tension. You can also try focusing your mind on a single object or point of concentration, such as the breath or a mantra, to help bring your attention into the present moment. Remember that the process of stilling the mind is a gradual one; it takes time and practice to develop this skill. But with patience and perseverance, you will achieve a deeper level of consciousness and connection with the universal mind.

After sharing his doubts and questions with Amma, the young brahmachari felt a sense of peace and clarity settle over his heart and mind. He prostrated before Amma, expressing his gratitude for the guidance and wisdom she had shared with him, and then went on his way to feed the cows. As he worked, he felt a new sense of purpose and focus. It was as if Amma's words had opened up new possibilities for him on his spiritual journey. And in his heart, he knew that he would continue to seek Amma's guidance and support as he moved forward, learning to still his mind and connect more deeply with the universal consciousness that lies within us all.

Commentary
In this moving conversation, Amma shares with an earnest disciple how to still the individual mind and connect with the universal mind.

The Role of Stillness
Amma emphasizes the crucial importance of stillness in connecting with the Divine. By quieting the mind and reducing mental chatter, we can cultivate the inner stillness that connects us with the Divine within and the world without.

The Benefits of Inner Stillness
The benefits of inner stillness include a greater sense of peace, clarity, and understanding. By cultivating inner stillness, we can reduce stress and anxiety, improve our focus and concentration, and deepen our understanding of ourselves and the world around us.

The Connection with the Universal Mind
Amma emphasizes the connection between inner stillness and the universal mind, which interconnects all things. By cultivating inner stillness, we can tap into this universal mind and gain a greater sense of oneness and mutual understanding with all beings.

Conclusion
In order to connect with the universal mind, inner stillness is essential. The benefits of inner stillness include greater peace, clarity, and understanding. By reducing mental noise and cultivating inner stillness, we can tap into the collective consciousness and gain a greater sense of unity with all that is.

***

49. Attachments
"Free from attachments to the past and worries about the future, child express themselves fully." – Amma

Once a sixty-five-year-old ashram resident, who had been dedicated to his sadhana and to his seva, came to Amma with a heavy heart. He had faithfully passed out tea and snacks during Devi Bhava to visitors for years on end. However, despite his dedication and efforts, he often found himself weighed down by worries and regrets about the past, which prevented him from fully enjoying the present moment and expressing himself freely. Seeking a solution to his inner struggles, he was hoping Amma could offer him solace and guidance.

As he poured out his heart to Amma, sharing his deepest fears and concerns with her, Amma listened patiently. Her gentle presence offered him a sense of calm and reassurance.

Ashram resident: Amma, I have been doing seva and sadhana in the ashram for many years now, but I find myself constantly worrying about the past and the future. I am not able to express myself fully and always feel weighed down by attachments.

Amma: My dear child, remember that the past and the future are only illusions. They do not exist in the present moment. Just like a child who lives in the present and expresses himself fully, we too must learn to let go of our attachments and worries. When we are free from these burdens, we can live in the present moment and express ourselves.

Ashram resident: But how do I let go of these attachments and worries, Amma?

Amma: Through meditation and self-reflection, we can learn to detach ourselves from our thoughts and emotions. Just like a child who is innocent and free, we too can cultivate the same innocence and freedom within ourselves. Let go of the past and the future, my child, and live fully in the present moment.

With gratitude in his heart, he bowed before Amma and left feeling renewed and reinvigorated. And, as he returned to his seva, he found himself able to smile and connect more fully with those around him, free from the burdens of the past and open to the possibilities of the present.

Commentary

Amma wants us to live in the present moment, free from attachments to the past and worries about the future. Her words point to the wisdom of children, who often live in the moment and express themselves fully.

Living in the Present Moment

Living in the present moment, free from attachments to the past and worries about the future, nurtures inner peace and contentment within.

The Wisdom of Children

By observing the way children approach life, we can learn to be present and fully engaged in our experiences. This is why Amma suggests we spend at least a little time with children each day.

Expressing Ourselves Fully

It is important to express ourselves fully. By letting go of attachments to the past and worries about the future, we can live more authentically and fully in the present moment.

Conclusion

Amma invites us to live in the present moment, like children, free from attachments to the past and worries about the future. Being present and fully engaged in our experiences, brings inner peace, contentment and authenticity into our lives.

***

50. Mind
"Ask yourself, 'Why do I feel so miserable living in the midst of life's joyful celebration?'" —Amma

Once, a group of youngsters came to see Amma at the ashram. As they sat in front of her, Amma looked at them with a gentle smile.

Amma: Ask yourself, "Living in the midst of life's joyful celebration, why do I feel so miserable?"

The youngsters looked at each other, perplexed.

Youth 1: Amma, what do you mean?

Amma: Life is meant to be lived joyfully, with love and compassion towards all. But often, we find ourselves feeling unhappy and discontented, even in the midst of joyful celebrations. This is because we are attached to our desires and expectations, and when they are not fulfilled, we feel miserable. We need to learn to let go of these attachments and live in the present moment with gratitude and love.

The youngsters listened intently.

Youth 2: But how do we do that, Amma?

Amma: By cultivating self-awareness and mindfulness. By observing our thoughts and emotions and understanding their root causes. By practicing meditation and other spiritual practices that help us connect with our inner self. This way, we can learn to let go of our attachments and live in a state of inner peace and joy.

Youth 3: Amma, I feel like I'm missing out on life. Everyone around me seems to be happy and enjoying themselves, but I feel so miserable inside. What can I do to change this?

Amma: You need to ask yourself why you feel that way. Are you constantly comparing yourself to others? Are you holding on to past hurts or regrets? Are you worried about the future?

Youth 2: Yes, we are all constantly comparing ourselves with each and worrying about the future. We also feel like we haven't accomplished anything significant in our lives.

Amma: It's important to remember that everyone's journey is unique, and everyone has their own challenges to overcome. Comparing yourself to others will only lead to feelings of inadequacy and misery. Instead, focus on your own journey and how you can make the most of it. As for feeling like, 'I haven't accomplished anything' remember that every small step you take towards your goals is an accomplishment in itself.

Remember, true happiness comes from within. Learn to live in the present moment and enjoy the simple pleasures of life. Don't let your worries and fears consume you. Instead, trust in the Divine and have faith that everything will work out for the best.

The youngsters nodded, taking in Amma's words with reverence and gratitude.

Commentary

Amma challenges us to reflect on why we often feel miserable even in the midst of life's joyful celebrations. Her words encourage us to examine our inner state and to look at the factors that may be contributing to our sense of unhappiness.

The Illusion of External Happiness

External happiness is an illusion; its very nature is fleeting and unreliable. Thus, even in the midst of joyful celebrations, we may still feel miserable.

Examining Our Inner State

Amma encourages us to examine our inner state and the factors that may be contributing to our sense of unhappiness. By reflecting on our thoughts, emotions, and beliefs, we can gain a greater understanding of the underlying causes of our unhappiness and take steps to address them.

The Importance of Inner Peace

By focusing on our inner state and working to cultivate inner peace, we invite lasting and fulfilling happiness into our lives, even in the midst of life's challenges.

Conclusion

Amma urges us to look at our inner state to find the factors that may be causing unhappiness for us. When we reflect and actively cultivate inner peace and contentment within, we can experience more lasting and fulfilling happiness.

***

51. Love

"Love is the most natural thing for humans. We should perform all our actions, from that center point of love." – Amma.

There was once a brahmachari working in the kitchen who was not fully committed to his duties. Instead of blowing the pipe to keep the fire going, thus ensuring that there was sufficient heat to cook, he was restless and distracted. He was often thinking of other things, and even snuck away to the beach to meditate from time to time.

One day, Amma visited the kitchen while this brahmachari should have been on duty. She noticed that the fire was not burning properly and that the heat was not sufficient for cooking. Without hesitation, she picked up the pipe and started blowing into it herself.

The brahmachari came back at that very moment.

Brahmachari: Amma, I am so sorry! I wasn't doing my seva properly. For some reason, I feel restless and distracted while working in the kitchen. It's hard for me to focus on blowing the pipe to keep the fire going.

Amma: My dear child, have you ever tried doing your work with love and devotion? Imagine that you are doing Pada Puja to your Ista Devatha. Focus on that act of worship and infuse your work with love. If you do this, you will find that your tasks become easier, and you will feel a deeper sense of purpose.

At that moment, several devotees rushed in to sit near Amma.

Devotee 1: Amma, I find it difficult to love everyone, especially those who have wronged me in the past. How can I practice love in such situations?

Amma: It's natural to feel hurt and angry when someone wrongs you. But holding onto those negative emotions will only hurt you more. Instead, try to forgive and let go of the past. Focus on the present moment and find something positive to appreciate in that person. When you practice love and forgiveness, you will feel lighter and more at peace.

Devotee 2: Amma, my problem is even worse. I struggle to love myself. I often feel unworthy and inadequate. What should I do?

Amma: My dear child, you are a precious and unique creation of God. You are worthy of love and respect, just as you are. When you start to feel negative thoughts about yourself, try to replace them with positive affirmations. Focus on your strengths and talents and be kind to yourself. When you practice self-love, you will radiate positive energy and attract more love into your life.

As the questions tapered off, the brahmachari approached Amma and prostrated.

Brahmachari: Amma from now on, I will keep the kitchen fire burning while meditating on my beloved deity.

Amma: My blessings are with you, my child. Remember, love is the key to happiness and fulfillment in life. Let it guide your thoughts, words, and actions always.

Commentary

Amma highlights the importance of love as a guiding principle in our lives. She emphasizes the naturalness of love and encourages us to remain immersed in it in all our actions.

The Naturalness of Love

Love is of fundamental importance to human beings. It is the universal emotion that transcends all cultural and societal boundaries, knitting us together as a world family.

Love as a Guiding Principle

Amma encourages us to make love a guiding principle in our lives. By imbuing all of our actions with love, we can cultivate greater compassion, empathy, and understanding for ourselves and others.

The Power of Love

Love holds the power to transform our lives and the world around us. It has the power to heal, unite, and inspire positive change in the world.

Conclusion

Love is the guiding principle of life; it is our own true nature. By cultivating love in our hearts, we can transform ourselves and the world around us.

***

52. Mind
"Learn to be considerate. Don't be obsessed with what you think is right." – Amma

During darshan, a devotee approached Amma with a question about how to accept others, especially when their beliefs or opinions differed from her own.

Devotee: Amma, I recently had a heated argument with a friend about spirituality. These days I'm having trouble accepting others when their beliefs or opinions differ from my own. How can I see the humanity in those who attack my beliefs?

Amma: My child, it's natural to feel attached to our own beliefs and opinions, but we must learn to be considerate of others. It's important to respect everyone's right to their own beliefs.

Devotee: But how do I do this, Amma. How do I begin to see the humanity in those who attack my deeply held convictions?

Amma: To see the humanity in others, we must first see it in ourselves. We are all connected; we are all children of the same Divine Consciousness. When we approach others with love and compassion, we are able to see beyond their beliefs to the essence of their being.

Devotee: Ok, Amma. That makes sense, but how can I experience this divine connection?
Amma: Try these four steps, and see if they help:

1. Start by practicing Self-awareness and mindfulness.
2. When you feel yourself becoming attached to your own beliefs, take a step back and breathe.
3. Ask yourself, 'Is this thought serving me or others'?
4. Approach the situation with love and compassion and see what unfolds.

The devotee humbly bowed her head and prostrated to Amma.

Amma: My child, remember that the path of spirituality is about opening our hearts and loving and serving others. When we can do this, we transcend our limited beliefs and connect with the divine consciousness that unites us.

The devotee felt a sense of relief and gratitude as she listened to Amma's words. She realized that she had been so obsessed with what she thought was right that she had lost sight of the bigger picture. As she left darshan, she felt inspired to practice compassion and kindness towards others no matter what they believed.

Commentary

Amma advises us to cultivate consideration for others and to avoid becoming obsessed with our own ideas of what is right. It is much more important to focus on empathy and understanding in our relationships.

The Importance of Consideration

When we take the time to understand where others are coming from, we are inviting the transformative power of love into the conversation.

Avoiding Obsession

Amma warns against becoming obsessed with our own ideas of what is right. Instead, we should remain open-minded and receptive.

Conclusion

Amma encourages us to cultivate consideration for others and to avoid becoming obsessed with our own idea of what is right. It is much healthier to invest our energy into empathic, meaningful relationships with others. By learning to be more considerate, we can become beacons of peace and harmony for others.

53. Mind

"When others get what they wish, we are sad. It's a disease of the mind that eats away our peace." – Amma

One day during darshan, a devotee approached Amma with a heavy heart. He expressed to Amma that he was feeling sad because his brother was doing exceptionally well in business.

Devotee: Amma, I'm feeling sad because my brother is doing well in his business. We have been competitive with each other since childhood, and I can't help but feel envious of his success. Please help me to overcome this feeling of envy.

Amma: My child, envy is a disease of the mind that eats away our peace. When we are focused on what others have, we lose sight of our own blessings and become unhappy. The key to overcoming envy is to focus on gratitude and contentment.

Devotee: But how can I do that, Amma? It's so hard to be grateful when I see my brother succeeding in areas where I've struggled.

Amma: Start by focusing on your own blessings, my child. Think of all the things you have to be grateful for - your health, your family, your friends, your job. When we focus on our blessings, we attract more blessings into our lives. Try to appreciate your brother's success without feeling threatened by it. When we celebrate the success of others, we create positive energy and open the door for our own success.

Devotee: That makes sense, Amma. I will try. I promise I will try.

Amma: Remember, my child, the path of spirituality is about letting go of our attachments and desires. When we focus on serving others and being content with what we have, we can find true peace and happiness.

Commentary

In this conversation, Amma addresses the negative emotions that can arise when we compare ourselves to others and become envious of their successes or achievements. The solution is choosing a positive and peaceful mindset.

The Negative Impact of Envy

Envy negatively impacts our emotional well-being. When we become envious of others, we inevitably experience feelings of sadness and frustration, which eat away at our peace of mind and create unnecessary stress in our lives.

The Importance of Mindfulness

Mindful is the key to cultivating a positive and peaceful mindset. By remaining aware of our thoughts and emotions, we can identify negative patterns of thinking and take steps to shift our focus towards more positive and uplifting perspectives.

Cultivating a Grateful Mindset

Rather than focusing on what others have, cultivate a mindset of gratitude and contentment. When we focus on the positive aspects of our lives and appreciate the blessings that we have, joy and fulfillment become our companions.

Conclusion

Envy undermines our emotional well-being, whereas, mindfulness and gratitude bring joy and contentment. By focusing on the blessings that we have, rather than comparing ourselves to others, we can enjoy peace and fulfillment.

***

54. Attitude

"If your attitude is positive and accepting, you live with God even while busy in the world." – Amma

During one of Amma's darshans, a man approached her with a heavy heart. The man was a bank manager and had been struggling with non-cooperative employees and anger issues. His negative attitude was affecting his relationships, and his employees were suffering as a result. One of his employees convinced him to seek Amma's guidance.

Man: Amma, I have been struggling with accepting things in my life, and it's affecting my relationships with people, especially at work. I am a bank manager, and I find it hard to cooperate with my employees. My negative attitude is causing problems for everyone. Can you help me find a way to become more accepting?

Amma: My child, acceptance is the key to living a peaceful life. When we accept what comes our way, we become more positive and open to opportunities. Acceptance also helps us to be kinder and more compassionate towards others.

Man: But Amma, how can I become more accepting when things don't go my way? How can I control my attitude?

Amma: Everything depends on your attitude, my child. If you can cultivate a positive and accepting attitude, you can live with God even while busy in the world. Try to focus on the positive aspects of your life and be grateful for what you have. When you encounter difficulties, try to see them as opportunities for growth and learning. Remember, nothing in life is permanent, and every experience is a chance to learn and grow.

Amma gave the man darshan. When he lifted his head up, he was visibly calmer.

Man: Amma I will try my best to focus on the positive and be more accepting of things that come my way.

Amma: Remember, my child, the path of spirituality is about self-improvement and service to others. When we live with a positive attitude of acceptance, we can bring more peace and happiness into our lives and the lives of those around us.

Commentary

Having a positive and accepting attitude towards life is essential. With such an attitude, we can experience a sense of connection to the divine, even as we go about our daily activities in the world.

The Power of Attitude

Our attitudes shape our experiences of the world around us. By cultivating a positive and accepting attitude, we can transform even the most challenging situations into opportunities for growth and learning.

Living with God

By adopting a positive and accepting attitude, we can experience a sense of connection to the divine in our everyday lives. Rather than viewing spirituality as separate from our daily activities, we begin to integrate it into our daily routines and find meaning and purpose in everything we do.

Finding Peace in the World

Amma clearly states that we can experience peace and connection to the divine even while living busy and active lives in the world. By adopting a positive and accepting attitude, we can find a peace within ourselves that accompanies us wherever we go.

Conclusion

Amma encourages us to develop a positive and accepting attitude towards life. With such an attitude, we can experience a sense of connection to the divine even in the midst of the busy world. By focusing on our attitude and finding ways to integrate spirituality into our daily lives, we can experience greater peace, purpose, and fulfillment in everything we do.

***

55. Wealth
"Money is not a problem, but unintelligent attachment to it is." – Amma

Some years ago, a businessman approached Amma during darshans with a heavy heart. He explained that he had invested a large sum of money in stocks and had lost it all, leaving him in a state of depression. His family was also feeling the strain of the financial loss. He asked Amma for guidance on how to cope with the situation.

Businessman: Amma, I am in a state of despair. I invested a lot of money in stocks, and I lost it all. I feel depressed, and my family is suffering. Can you please guide me? What should I do?

Amma: My child, money is not a problem, but unintelligent attachment to it is. It is important to use money wisely and to cultivate detachment towards it.

Businessman: But Amma, I thought I was investing wisely. I never expected this to happen.

Amma: Investing in the stock market is always a risk, my child. It is important to be aware of this fact and not become too attached to the outcome. You should approach your finances with a balanced perspective and not let your emotions cloud your judgment.

Businessman: I understand, Amma. But how should I cope with this loss?

Amma: The most important thing is not to give in to despair, my child. You should remain hopeful and optimistic in difficult times. Remember that nothing in life is permanent, that this too shall pass.

Businessman: Thank you, Amma. I will take your guidance to heart and try to learn from my mistakes.

Amma: Always remember, son, that the real wealth in life lies in cultivating love, compassion, and detachment. Money is just a means to an end, and it should never become an obsession.

Commentary

Amma wants us to have a healthy relationship with money. She says that money itself is not the problem, that attachment to it and misuse of it are the real source of trouble.

Money and Attachment

In Amma's view, the real problem with money is the attachment we develop towards it, either because we are obsessed with accumulating wealth or because we use money as a measure of our self-worth. This attachment can lead to greed, selfishness, and a lack of compassion for others.

The Importance of Balance

Rather than rejecting money altogether, Amma suggests that we find a healthy balance in our relationship with it. We appreciate money as a means to meet our family's basic needs, while understanding that money alone cannot bring us lasting happiness and fulfillment.

The Path to Freedom

Amma's words suggests that the path to true freedom lies in letting go of our attachment to money and recognizing its limitations. By cultivating a deeper sense of inner peace and contentment, we can find happiness and fulfillment in life, no matter what our financial circumstances.

Conclusion

Amma challenges us to examine our relationship with money and to cultivate a more balanced and healthy attitude towards it. By recognizing that money is not inherently good or bad, we can avoid the pitfalls of attachment and find a greater sense of inner freedom.

***

56. Charity
"It is through giving that we progress on the spiritual path."
— Amma

During one of Amma's satsangs, a family of four came to listen to her teachings. The husband, a miserly man, had always objected to his wife and children giving charity to the needy. Despite being a well-off family, he was not willing to part with his money. However, his wife and children had convinced him to come to Amma's ashram and to listen to her teachings about the importance of giving. Amma, as always, received them with a warm smile.

Amma: Welcome, my children. What brings you here today?

Wife: Amma, my kids and I brought my husband to you today. He does not understand the importance of charity and the joy it brings.

Amma: Ah, I see. Can you tell me why you don't believe in giving, my son?

Husband: Amma, I work very hard for my money. I don't want to just give it away to anyone who asks for it. It's not easy to earn money these days.

Amma: I understand, my son. But remember, we are not just physical beings, but spiritual beings as well. And it is through giving that we progress on the spiritual path. When we give, we not only help others, but we also purify our own mind and heart.

Husband: But Amma, I see people taking advantage of others' generosity all the time. I don't want to be a fool.

Amma: Giving is not about being foolish, my son. It is about having compassion and empathy for those who are less fortunate. You can always be discerning and give wisely. And remember, it is not about how much you give, but about the intention behind it.

Daughter: Amma, my brother and I feel so happy when we give to the poor. We know it's a small gesture, but it makes a big difference in others' lives.

Son: Yes, Amma. I think my father should try it too. It might make him happy.

Amma: That's wonderful to hear, my children. Giving should come from the heart, and it should bring joy and happiness. My son, if you're willing to try, I suggest you start small. Give something to someone in need and see how it makes you feel. And always remember, money is not a problem, but unintelligent attachment to it is.

Commentary

Amma suggests we learn to give, if we want to progress on the spiritual path. In fact, generosity and selflessness are essential qualities on the path to enlightenment.

The Power of Giving

Giving is a powerful way to cultivate the qualities of compassion, selflessness, and generosity. By giving to others, we can develop a deeper sense of empathy and connectedness, which can help us to overcome our own selfish desires and attachments.

Giving and Gratitude

Giving can also be a way to express gratitude for the blessings we have received. When we share our resources with others, we are acknowledging the interconnectedness of all beings and the ways in which we all depend on one another for our well-being.

Giving and Spiritual Progress

Amma emphasizes that giving is an essential part of the spiritual path. Through acts of kindness and generosity, we can overcome our ego-driven desires and move closer to a state of selflessness.

Conclusion

In this conversation, Amma challenges us to embrace the power of giving. By cultivating a spirit of generosity and selflessness, we not only benefit others, but also develop positive qualities within ourselves and move closer to our spiritual goals.

***

57. Compassion

"Consoling a miserable soul, wiping the tears of a crying person is greater than any worldly achievement." – Amma

While visiting a nearby village, Amma came across a family that was mourning the loss of their son, who had committed suicide by jumping into the backwaters. Amma offered words of comfort and solace and shared the family's grief and sorrow right alongside them. Amma's heart was heavy as she left the home of the grieving family. The brahmacharis accompanying her were in deep contemplation as they walked back to the ashram.

One of them spoke.

Brahmachari 1: Amma, what is the benefit of consoling someone in grief? How does it help us to progress spiritually?

Amma looked at him with compassion.

Amma: When you console a miserable soul or wipe away the tears of a crying person, this act of kindness is far greater than any worldly achievement. It helps you to develop empathy and compassion, and these qualities are essential for spiritual growth.

Brahmachari 2: But Amma, what if we console them and they don't even remember us or appreciate our efforts?

Amma: *(smiling)* That is not the point. We don't console a suffering soul to be rewarded or recognized. We should do it simply out of love and compassion for our fellow beings.

Brahmachari 3: But Amma, what if we ourselves are going through a difficult time. How can we console others then?

Amma: Son, we all go through difficult times. But even in those moments, we can offer a kind word or an attentive ear to someone else who is suffering. By helping others, we also help ourselves to heal and find meaning in our own struggles.

The brahmacharis listened to Amma's words with reverence and gratitude. They now realized that consoling someone in grief is not just an act of kindness, but also a powerful tool for their own spiritual growth.

Commentary
Amma models the importance of comforting and consoling those who are suffering every day. She suggests that we help others in their times of need as well. If we can do this, we have will have achieved something far greater than any worldly achievement.

Compassion and Empathy
Our interactions with others should be guided by empathy and compassion. When we put ourselves in the shoes of those who are suffering, we can better understand their pain and provide them with the comfort and support they need.

Service and Selflessness
We should strive to comfort others with an attitude of service and selflessness. By putting the needs of others before our own, we can make a meaningful difference in their lives and show them that they are not alone in their struggles.

Spiritual Significance
Consoling those who are suffering is a spiritual practice. By offering comfort and support, we embody the qualities of love, compassion, and selflessness that are at the very heart of spiritual traditions around the world.

Conclusion
With these words Amma challenges us to prioritize empathy, compassion, service, and selflessness in our interactions with others. By consoling those who are suffering, we can make a meaningful difference and progress on the spiritual path. Amma suggests that this type of service and selflessness is a far greater accomplishment than we can imagine.

Dialogues with Amma

***

58. Righteousness
"If you perform your work viewing it as your dharma, your actions become sacred." – Amma

As Amma was discussing the sacred nature of work with some devotees, she received news of a terrible accident in Tamil Nadu. A short circuit in a firecracker factory had caused many fatalities and injuries. Upon hearing this news, Amma announced her plan to help the victims and their families.

Amma: The accident in Tamil Nadu is a terrible tragedy. We must help the families in any way we can.

Devotee 1: But Amma, what can we do to help them?

Amma: We will provide free treatment in AIMS Kochi to the victims who were injured in the accident, and we will educate the children who lost their parents.

The room fell silent for a long time. Then a devotee quietly asked a question.

Devotee 2: Amma it may not be appropriate to ask now, but how can we view our work as sacred as you were saying earlier? Those working in the factory all lost their lives while on the job.

Amma: If we perform our work with a sense of duty and responsibility, and with the intention to serve others, then our actions become sacred. It's not just about the work itself, but our attitude towards it.

Devotee 3: Amma, sometimes we may not find meaning or purpose in our work. How can we still view it as sacred?

Amma: Every job or task has its own importance in the larger scheme of things. Even if you do not see the impact of your work directly, know that it is contributing to the overall well-being of society. It's important to approach every task with a positive attitude and a sense of service.

Commentary

After responding to the terrible accident in the factory, Amma turns back to the discussion about work. She encourages us to view our work as sacred and to consider it as our dharma, our sacred duty.

Understanding Dharma

Amma highlights the importance of acting according to dharma, which is often translated as duty, righteousness, or virtue. Dharma is a central concept in Hinduism, Buddhism, and Jainism. It refers to one's moral and ethical responsibilities.

Work as Sacred

By viewing our work as our dharma, our actions become sacred. When we work with noble intentions, even the most mundane of tasks can become meaningful and significant.

Mindful Action

In order to make our work sacred, we must act in a mindful and intentional manner. By bringing our full attention and awareness to our work, we can rest assured that we are fulfilling our dharma.

Conclusion

Amma challenges us to view our work as sacred and to consider it our dharma. By doing so, our actions, even mundane tasks, become meaningful and significant. This requires a mindful and intentional approach to our work, and an understanding of our moral and ethical responsibilities.

***

59. Education
"There are two types of education: education for livelihood and education for life. " –Amma

The grand auditorium was filled with distinguished guests, scholars, and professors from various universities. The stage was decorated with colorful flowers and traditional lamps. The atmosphere was reverential as everyone awaited the arrival of Amma. She was about to be awarded an honorary doctorate for her contributions to society.

Finally, the moment arrived, and Amma gracefully walked onto the stage to receive the award. She humbly accepted the honor and addressed the audience with her usual warmth and compassion. She spoke of the importance of education, saying that education is not just for earning a livelihood, it's also for learning how to live a good life. Amma went on to emphasize the need for holistic education that encompasses the physical, mental, emotional, and spiritual aspects of each student.

As her words echoed throughout the auditorium, the professors listened attentively, feeling inspired by her message. Amma stressed the importance of living a life of service and compassion, and of recognizing the oneness in the world.

Professor A: Namaste, Amma. It's an honor to have you here with us. Congratulations on your honorary doctorate.

Amma: I feel that this recognition is not only for me, but for all those who have dedicated their lives to serving others. I believe that education is one of the most important ways we can serve humanity.

Professor B: Yes, education is crucial for a successful career and a better future.

Amma: Indeed. That is true, but I believe there are two types of education: education for livelihood and education for life. While education for livelihood is important, we also need education for life that helps us develop compassion, empathy, and self-awareness.

Professor C: That's an interesting perspective. Can you tell us more about education for life?

Amma: Education for life teaches us how to live in harmony with ourselves, others, and the environment. It involves developing the qualities of the heart, such as kindness, gratitude, and forgiveness. It also cultivates a sense of oneness with the world around us and helps us recognize that we are all interconnected and interdependent.

Professor D: That's a beautiful vision. How can we incorporate education for life into our educational institutions?

Amma: One way is by integrating holistic health practices into the curriculum, such as yoga, meditation, and mindfulness. These practices help students develop self-awareness and emotional regulation, which are essential for their well-being and success. Another way is to encourage community service and social action, which help students develop compassion and a sense of responsibility towards others.

Professor E: That's very inspiring, Amma. Thank you for sharing your wisdom with us.

Amma: Thank you for your kind attention.

The professors felt deeply moved by her words and felt grateful for the opportunity to listen to such an enlightened soul. The ceremony concluded with thunderous applause as everyone stood to express their appreciation for Amma and her teachings.

Commentary

In her address, Amma makes a distinction between education for livelihood and education for life. She suggests that while education for livelihood is important, it should not be the sole focus of our educational pursuits.

Education for Livelihood

Amma acknowledges the importance of education for livelihood, education that prepares individuals for specific careers and professions. This type of education is necessary for individuals to earn a living and support themselves and their families.

Education for Life

In addition to this, Amma suggests that we focus on education for life. This type of education develops moral and ethical values that contribute to the enrichment of both the individual student and society at large.

Conclusion

Amma is advocating a more balanced approach to education. While education for livelihood is important, it should not be the sole focus of our educational pursuits. Instead, we should strive to balance our educational approach and integrate personal growth and development in our educational institutions.

***

60. Nature
"It is the duty of human beings to protect all living creatures, seeing Nature as our mother." –Amma

Amma, known for her love for all living creatures, was once given a baby elephant named Ram. She absolutely loved to spend time with him. Over the years, she has also been given several dogs: Tumaban, Bhakti, Rishi, Kiser with whom she also shared a deep connection. These days, Amma's new canine companion is named Shakti. Throughout her life, Amma has often played with birds, and even kissed trees, plants, and flowers, as an expression of her reverence for nature. During her sadhana days, when she dove into intense spiritual practice, two stray dogs would loyally bring food packets to her from nowhere, and an eagle would drop fish from the ocean near her feet. Even now, Amma fondly recalls these experiences.

Once, a brahmachari asked Amma how to connect with nature, which led to a casual conversation between Amma and the brahmachari.

Brahmachari: Amma, I am struggling to connect with nature and to live a more holistic life. Can you guide me?

Amma: Yes, my child. Nature is not separate from us. It is our mother. It is our duty as human beings to protect all living creatures and to see nature as our own. When we realize this, we automatically become one with nature. We start to feel the pain of every living creature and take actions to protect them.

Brahmachari: But Amma, how can I connect with nature on a daily basis? I live in a city and don't have much access to nature.

Amma: You don't need to be surrounded by forests to connect with nature. You can start by being mindful of the little things around you. Observe the tree and plant near you, even if it's just a small one growing through a crack in the pavement. Listen to the birds chirping, notice the clouds moving across the sky. When you start to appreciate the beauty of nature in everything around you, you will naturally start to feel a connection with it.

Brahmachari: Thank you, Amma. I will try to observe and listen.

Amma: That is all I ask, my child. Remember, we are all part of the same ecosystem, and it is our duty to protect it for the benefit of all living creatures.

Commentary

Amma encourages us to protect all living creatures and to recognize nature as our mother. She suggests that it is our duty as human beings to protect and care for the natural world around us.

Protecting Living Creatures

It is our duty to protect all living creatures. This includes not only humans, but also animals and plants. By recognizing the inherent value of all living beings, we can work towards creating a more compassionate world.

Seeing Nature as Our Mother

Amma suggests that we see nature as our mother. This perspective encourages us to see the interconnectedness of all living things and to treat the natural world with the same care and respect that we would give to a beloved family member.

Our Duty as Human Beings

Amma emphasizes that it is our responsibility to protect all living creatures and to care for the natural world.

Conclusion

Amma urges us to protect all living creatures and to recognize nature as our mother. By embracing this perspective and recognizing our duty to care for the natural world, we can work towards creating a better world for all living creatures.

Dialogues with Amma

***

61. Japa

"Chant your mantra while engaged in work. This way, the mind will be continuously focused on Him." – Amma

Amma sat on the stage, adorned with flowers and a radiant smile, as the devotees from Rajasthan gathered around her for Devi Bhava darshan. Her eyes scanned the crowd, taking in their eager faces and hopeful eyes. Suddenly, she spotted a young boy sitting among them, his lips moving silently as he chanted his mantra with deep concentration.

Amma: Look at this boy, chanting his mantra with such sincerity. It is so beautiful to see someone focused on the Divine like that.

Devotee 1: Amma, I also try to chant my mantra regularly, but sometimes it's hard to focus when I'm at work or doing other things.

Amma: That is understandable, but if you can chant your mantra while you work, it will help keep your mind focused on the Divine. It is like the camel in the desert, who needs to be well-cared for so that it can cross the hot sands. In the same way, we need to take care of our mind and keep it focused on God.

Devotee 2: But Amma, what if we have to do work that requires a lot of concentration, like solving a math problem or writing a report?

Amma: Of course, there may be times when you need to focus on your work with your full attention. But even then, you can keep a part of your mind focused on your mantra. It is like a candle flame that is always burning in the background, reminding you of the Divine.

Devotee 3: Amma, what if we don't have a mantra? How can we find one?

Amma: There are many mantras that you can choose from, depending on your tradition or your personal preference. But the most important thing is to choose a mantra that resonates with your heart and to chant it with sincerity and devotion. If you don't have a mantra yet, you can ask your spiritual teacher or explore until you find one that feels right for you.

The devotees took Amma's words to heart and left darshan inspired.

Commentary

Amma suggests that we can maintain a continuous connection with the Divine by chanting our mantra while engaged in work. By doing so, we can keep our mind focused on God and maintain a sense of inner peace throughout the day.

Chanting Your Mantra

We can maintain our connection with the Divine by chanting our mantra. By repeating this sacred sound, we can anchor our awareness in the present moment and maintain a sense of inner peace.

Being Engaged in Work

Amma advises us to chant our mantra even while engaged in work. We don't need to set aside special time for this spiritual practice. By chanting wherever we are, we infuse our daily activities with the presence of the Divine

Maintaining a Continuous Connection

Chanting our mantra throughout the day will help us to stay focused, calm, and centered even in the midst of life's challenges and distractions.

Conclusion

Amma suggests that we chant our mantra all day long, even while engaged in work. Doing so connects us to the present moment and the Divine. This will help us stay focused, calm, and centered no matter what is going on in the world outside.

Amma talks with Devotees

***

62. Behavior

"Keep constant awareness. Make a conscious effort to speak good words and perform good actions. Practice patience and compassion." – Amma

One day, one of Amma's devotees expressed doubt about the practicality of living a kind, compassionate life in the outside world.

Devotee: Amma, I have been saying good words and performing good actions as you have taught us. But back home in the world, people take advantage of my kindness. How can I continue to do good without being taken advantage of?

Amma: My dear child, I understand your concerns. The world can be a challenging place, and it can be difficult to maintain our values in the face of adversity. However, we must remember that our actions are not for others, but for ourselves. We perform good deeds and speak good words not to please others, but to cultivate goodness within ourselves. This practice helps us to maintain a pure heart and a clear mind, which is essential for our own spiritual growth.

We must understand that the actions of others are not within our control. We cannot change how others perceive us or how they react to our goodness. However, we can control our own actions and responses. Therefore, it is crucial to remain patient and compassionate towards others, even when they do not reciprocate with kindness.

Always remember, our good deeds and words create positive energy that radiates out into the world, making it a better place. Even if people do not immediately recognize or appreciate our efforts, the positive impact is still there. So, my child, continue to do good and have faith that it will make a difference, even if you cannot see it right away.

The devotee humbly prostrated

Devotee: Amma, thank you so much for clearing up my doubt. I now understand that doing good is not about others but about improving myself. I will try my very best to remain patient and compassionate even in the face of adversity.

Commentary

Amma's teachings on the importance of maintaining goodness, patience, and compassion, even in the face of adversity, are essential in today's world. By staying true to these values, we can cultivate positive energy within ourselves and make a positive impact on the world, even in these challenging times.

The Power of Words and Actions

Amma highlights the impact our words and actions can have on those around us. It is important to be mindful of the consequences of our actions and the effect our behavior has on others. By choosing our words and actions wisely, we can positively influence those around us and create a ripple effect of kindness and compassion.

Practicing Patience and Compassion

Amma encourages us to cultivate patience and compassion in our daily lives. Patience is essential when dealing with challenging situations or difficult people. Compassion allows us to see others with understanding and empathy, rather than judgment and criticism.

Cultivating Awareness in Everyday Life

Amma emphasizes the importance of being aware of our thoughts, words, and actions in everyday life. By cultivating mindfulness, we can become more conscious of the impact our behavior has on others and make more intentional choices. This awareness can also help us recognize and change negative thought patterns, leading to greater inner peace and fulfillment.

Conclusion

Amma's teachings remind us of the power inherent in our words and actions, and the importance of cultivating patience, compassion, and awareness. If we choose wisely, together we can create a more positive and harmonious world both for ourselves and those around us.

***

63. Gratitude

"Thankfulness is a humble, open and prayerful attitude that helps you receive more of God's grace." —Amma

One day, a brahmachari approached Amma to complain because no one ever thanked him for his hard work. This brahmachari had just had a fight with an inmate who did not go to get water for the ashram like he was supposed to. Instead, the brahmachari did the work and went to the other side to bring the water himself. Despite working hard every day, he felt unappreciated and upset.

Amma: What happened, my child? Why are you upset?

Brahmachari: Amma, I am feeling angry and frustrated. I work so hard every day, but no one appreciates me. Today, I had an argument with an inmate because he did not finish his task, and I had to do extra work. You talk about gratitude so often, but why should I be thankful when no one ever thanks me?

Amma: My child, I understand that you are feeling hurt, and you feel unappreciated. But remember, thankfulness is not about expecting others to thank you. It is about having a humble and open attitude towards life. When you are thankful, you open yourself up to receive more of God's grace. When you are humble, you become a channel for God's love and compassion to flow through you.

Brahmachari: But how can I be thankful when no one appreciates me?

Amma: Thankfulness is not about being thanked by others. It is about being grateful for the opportunities that life gives you. You are here to serve others and to do God's work. Whether others appreciate you or not, you can still be thankful for the chance to serve. And when you serve with a thankful heart, you will find that your work becomes more meaningful, and you will receive more of God's blessings.

Brahmachari: Amma. I will try. I will really try to be more grateful.

Amma: Remember, my child, that thankfulness is a prayerful attitude that opens you up to receive more of God's grace. May you always be filled with gratitude and love.

Commentary

Thankfulness involves recognizing and appreciating the blessings in one's life, no matter how small they may seem.

The Importance of Thankfulness

Amma believes that thankfulness is an essential quality that helps individuals to lead happy lives. By recognizing and appreciating the blessings in our lives, we can develop a more positive outlook and cultivate a sense of gratitude.

The Relationship Between Thankfulness and Grace

Thankfulness is a prayerful attitude that opens our heart to receive more of God's grace. When we cultivate a thankful attitude, we become more receptive to the blessings that God has in store for us.

How to Cultivate Thankfulness

Amma suggests that we can cultivate gratitude by focusing on the present moment, being mindful of the blessings in our life, and expressing gratitude towards others. By making gratitude a habit, we will know greater peace.

The Benefits of Thankfulness

Practicing thankfulness has numerous benefits including reduced stress levels, improved mental health, and greater happiness. When we focus on the blessings in our lives, we develop a more positive outlook and become more resilient in the face of challenges.

Conclusion

Gratitude is a crucial attitude that can help us to receive more of God's grace. By recognizing and appreciating the blessings in our lives, we can cultivate a more positive outlook and experience greater contentment. The practice of gratitude requires a mindful, prayerful attitude, but the benefits are well worth the effort.

***

64. Attitude
"Look carefully to see what is of value in others and respect that." –Amma

During Amma's birthday celebrations, many volunteers come forward to perform tireless seva throughout the program. While working together, frictions are bound to arise, but Amma's teachings inspire each sevite to see the good in others and to respect that.

Before this particular birthday, Amma reminded the group of volunteers to follow this approach, and it brought a sense of harmony and unity to the team. Such is the power of Amma's teachings, which transform individuals and communities for the better.

Volunteer 1: Amma, we want to thank you for encouraging us to find the good in each other and to respect that. It has really helped us work together and avoid conflicts during this busy birthday celebration.

Amma: My dear children, I am so happy to hear that you are seeing the value in each other and working in harmony.

Volunteer 2: Yes, Amma. It was not always easy, but whenever we started to feel frustrated or upset with each other, we remembered your words and tried to see the good in each other.

Amma: That is wonderful to hear. Remember, my children, that every person has their own unique qualities and strengths. By respecting and valuing those qualities, we can work together in a spirit of cooperation and love.

Volunteer 3: Amma, thank you for guiding us in this way. We hope to carry these teachings with us and apply them in our daily lives.

Amma: I pray you all continue to cultivate this attitude of respect and appreciation for others. May it bring more peace and happiness to your lives and to the world around you.

Commentary

Amma's words inspire us to find the best in others. Such an attitude can help us to keep a positive attitude and to work together in harmony.

Recognizing Value in Others

Amma encourages us to observe and recognize the unique strengths and talents of others. By acknowledging and valuing their abilities and qualities, we learn to appreciate and respect all those who come into our lives

Respecting Others

Respect is a fundamental aspect in healthy relationships. Amma teaches us to respect others whatever their age, gender, ethnicity, or social status. Through respect, individuals can foster positive relationships and promote harmonious communities

Benefits of Respecting Others

By respecting others, we cultivate compassion, empathy, and kindness. When we recognize the value in others, we also enhance our own self-awareness and self-esteem. By promoting a culture of respect, we can build a more inclusive and supportive society.

Conclusion

In conclusion, Amma's words highlight the importance of recognizing and respecting the value of others. By acknowledging their strengths and abilities, we contribute to a culture lit up with respect, positive relationships and harmony.

***

65. Nature
"By living in harmony with Nature one gains a healthy mind and body." – Amma

One day, Amma noticed that a brahmachari was overcome by laziness and was not doing any physical work at all. She advised him to start seed ball planting and explained to him how it could benefit his mind and body.

Amma: Son, seed ball planting is an excellent way to serve nature while taking care of your own physical and mental well-being. It just involves making small balls of soil and seeds, which can then be thrown or placed in barren areas. Over time, these seeds will germinate and grow into beautiful plants, creating a green and healthy environment.

The Brahmachari was inspired by Amma's words and immediately took up seed ball planting. He found that by serving nature, he felt a deep sense of purpose and connectedness with the world around him. The brahmachari returned to Amma to thank her.

Brahmachari: Amma, I am so grateful for your guidance. After you told me about seed ball planting, I started doing it, and it has been such a transformative experience for me. Not only am I more physically fit, but I feel a sense of peace and joy in my mind.

Amma: I am happy to hear that, my child. Nature has so much to offer us, and it is important that we nurture her in return. When we work in harmony with nature, both physical and mental well-being improve.

Brahmachari: Yes, I have realized that. It feels so good to be doing something to save the soil and protect the environment.

Amma: That is the beauty of it. When we serve nature, we are also serving ourselves and future generations. Keep up the good work, my child, and continue to live in harmony with nature.

Commentary
The Significance of Living in Harmony with Nature

Amma believes that humans have a responsibility to protect the environment and to live in harmony with nature. She stresses that the earth is not just a resource for humans to exploit but is a living entity that sustains all life. She encourages people to respect nature and to live in harmony with it.

How Living in Harmony with Nature Can Improve Mental Health

Amma teaches that living in harmony with nature can have a positive impact on mental health. When people connect with nature, they feel a sense of peace and harmony. This connection can reduce stress, anxiety and depression, and can improve overall well-being.

The Benefits of a Healthy Mind and Body

A healthy mind and body are essential for living a fulfilling life. When people live in harmony with nature, they can enjoy a healthy diet, fresh air, and physical activity. This can help them lead a happy life blessed with good physical and mental health.

Practical Ways to Live in Harmony with Nature

Amma suggests various ways to live in harmony with nature, which include reducing waste, using eco-friendly products, conserving water and energy, planting trees and supporting environmental causes.

Amma's Message of Compassion Towards All Living Beings

Amma believes that all living beings are interconnected and that humans have a responsibility to treat animals with compassion and respect. She encourages people to adopt a vegetarian or vegan lifestyle and to support animal rights causes.

Conclusion

Amma emphasize the importance of respecting and protecting the environment. By living in harmony with nature, people can improve their mental and physical health and contribute to a healthier planet. Amma's message of compassion towards all living beings encourages people to adopt a kinder and more compassionate lifestyle.

***

66. Selfless service
"Purify the mind through selfless service." —Amma

During the COVID pandemic, the world was in crisis and in dire need of humanitarian aid. In the face of this adversity, the ashram, led by Amma, stepped forward to serve those in need. The Ashram organized the distribution of food kits consisting of essential items such as rice, sugar, dal, chili, coconuts etc., to help those in distress across Kerala. The selfless service of the Ashram volunteers brought relief to many households in the state and brought hope in a time of despair. Amma's teachings on the purification of the mind through selfless service were truly exemplified by the actions of her disciples.

As a group of disciples returned from distributing supplies in Haridwar, Amma took time to ask about their experience.

Disciple 1: Amma, we are amazed at how we were able to distribute kits to so many households during this pandemic. It was a huge task, but we were able to accomplish it through your grace.

Amma: Yes, my dear child. The purification of the mind through selfless service is the essence of our spiritual practice. When we serve others with love and compassion, we not only help them but also purify our own minds.

Disciple 2: Amma, we were able to distribute kits to so many remote areas where people were struggling to get basic necessities. It was a very humbling experience for us.

Amma: Yes, my child. It is in serving those who are most in need that we can truly understand the value of selfless service. Always remember that the more you give, the more you will receive.

Disciple 3: Amma, we faced many challenges during the distribution, but we were able to overcome them through teamwork and determination.

Amma: That is wonderful, my child. When we work together as a team with a common goal, we can achieve great things. Always remember that in serving others, we are serving the Divine.

Disciple 4: Amma, we are so grateful for this experience. It has been life-changing!

Amma: My daughter, the opportunity to serve is a great blessing. It is through service that we can truly experience the joy and fulfillment of life. May you continue to serve others with love and compassion, and may your actions always be guided by the Divine.

Commentary
The Concept of Selfless Service

Selfless service, seva, is the act of serving others without any expectation of personal gain. It is a fundamental principle in many spiritual traditions. The underlying idea is that by serving others, we serve a higher power and, ultimately, ourselves.

How Selfless Service Purifies the Mind

Selfless service is a powerful tool for purifying the mind. When we serve others without any expectation of reward, we free ourselves from selfish desires and attachments. This helps to quiet the mind and helps us cultivate a sense of inner peace and contentment.

Examples of Selfless Service

Selfless service can take many forms, from volunteering at a local charity to simply helping a neighbor in need. Some examples of selfless service include:

–Volunteering at a homeless shelter or food bank
–Donating time at a community garden or park
–Tutoring a child or teaching a class at a community center
–Helping an elderly or disabled person with household tasks
–Supporting a friend or family member in need

The Benefits of Selfless Service

In addition to purifying the mind, selfless service has many other benefits. It can help to build a sense of community and connection with others, promote feelings of empathy and compassion, and provide a sense of purpose and fulfillment.

How to Incorporate Selfless Service into Your Life

Participating in selfless service can be as simple as helping those you come across in your day-to-day life. It can also involve seeking out volunteer opportunities in your community or joining a service-oriented organization. The key is to approach service with an open heart and a willingness to give of yourself without expecting anything in return.

Conclusion

Amma's teachings on selfless service highlight the importance of putting others before ourselves and finding fulfillment in serving a higher purpose. By incorporating selfless service into our lives, we not only help others but also ourselves.

***

67. Witness

"Develop the ability to stand back as a witness to your thoughts. This will make your mind strong." – Amma

A group of disciples had been practicing penance in Haridwar for some time, hoping to make spiritual progress. Despite their efforts, they were not advancing. They decided to visit Amma for guidance and advice. The conversation turned to witness consciousness.

Disciple 1: Amma, what do you mean when you advise us to stand back as a witness to our thoughts?

Amma: Son, it means observing your thoughts without getting attached to them. Instead of getting carried away by your thoughts and emotions, simply observe them without any judgment or reaction.

Disciple 2: How can this make us spiritually strong, Amma?

Amma: When you observe your thoughts from a distance, you become aware of the patterns and tendencies of your mind. You start to see how your mind works and how it influences your behavior. This awareness helps you to take control of your mind and not be controlled by it.

Disciple 3: Can you give us a practical example, Amma?

Amma: Sure. Let's say you're feeling angry about something. Instead of acting out of anger, you observe your thoughts and feelings without getting caught up in them. You might notice that your anger is triggered by a particular situation or person. By observing your thoughts, you can gain clarity into why you are feeling angry and how you can respond in a more constructive way.

Disciple 4: How can we develop this witness attitude, Amma?

Amma: It takes practice, son, but the more you practice observing your thoughts, the easier it becomes. You can start by taking a few minutes each day to sit quietly, observing your thoughts without judgment. You can also practice mindfulness throughout your day by paying attention to your thoughts and emotions as they arise.

Disciple 5: Thank you, prostrations to you Amma for your guidance. We will develop this witness attitude to gain clarity and to move forward

Amma: You are most welcome. Remember, the discriminating mind is like a muscle. The more you exercise it, the stronger it becomes.

Commentary
The Importance of Self-Awareness

Amma highlights the importance of self-awareness in spiritual growth. It is the foundation of any spiritual practice and requires constant effort. Without self-awareness, we are unable to witness our thoughts and actions objectively.

The Power of Witnessing Thoughts

By standing back and observing our thoughts, we can gain a deeper understanding of our mind and its workings. This helps us to detach from our thoughts and emotions, so we are not overwhelmed by them.

Strengthening the Mind

The mind is like a muscle that needs to be exercised to stay strong. Observing our thoughts regularly helps us to develop this ability and strengthens our mind. As we become more self-aware, we are better equipped to handle the challenges of life.

The Benefits of a Strong Mind

A strong mind enables us to stay calm and composed during trials, helps us make better decisions, and leads to a more fulfilling life. It also helps us to cultivate a deeper sense of inner peace and happiness.

Conclusion

Developing the ability to observe our thoughts and emotions from a distance is crucial for spiritual growth and personal development. Through regular practice, we can strengthen our mind and cultivate a deeper sense of self-awareness, fulfillment and peace.

***

68. Nature

"When humanity serves Nature, Nature serves humanity. When we serve animals and plants, they serve us in return."

—Amma

Once, a group of nature lovers from Himachal came to Amma seeking her guidance. They had been trekking in the deep summits and were reflecting on how to give back to nature, as it had given them so much. They recognized the importance of mutual care and responsibility in preserving our natural environment.

Nature Lover 1: Amma, we love spending time in nature, but we are concerned about the damage humans are causing to the environment. What can we do to help?

Amma: My dear child, it is essential to understand that humanity and nature are interconnected. When we serve nature, nature serves humanity. One of the best ways to help the environment is by serving animals and plants. When we take care of them, they, in turn, take care of us.

Nature Lover 2: Can you give us an example, Amma?

Amma: Let's say you plant a tree. The tree will provide shade, oxygen, and food for many animals, birds, and insects. These creatures, in turn, help to pollinate plants, spread seeds, and keep pests under control. By planting one tree, you are creating a whole ecosystem that benefits both humans and nature.

Nature Lover 3: But how can we serve animals and plants, Amma?

Amma: There are many ways to serve animals and plants. You can plant trees, create habitats for wildlife, feed birds and animals, and reduce your use of plastic and other harmful materials. You can also participate in conservation efforts and spread awareness about environmental issues.

Nature Lover 4: Thank you for your guidance, Amma. We will do our best to serve nature, animals, and plants and to protect our planet.

Amma: Wonderful, my children! Remember, we are all stewards of this beautiful planet, and it is our responsibility to protect and preserve it for future generations. May your love for nature inspire others to join in this important work.

Commentary
Serving Nature Benefits Humans

Amma teaches that when humans serve nature, nature reciprocates by serving humanity. Protecting the environment benefits humans in numerous ways and ensures a healthy and sustainable future for generations to come.

Humans and Nature Should Coexist

Amma suggests that humans should not see themselves as separate from nature, but as a part of it. A harmonious relationship between humans and nature is crucial for the survival of them both. By recognizing our interdependence, we can work towards a mutually beneficial relationship.

Importance of Preserving the Environment

Amma emphasizes the importance of preserving the environment. Human activities such as deforestation, pollution, and exploitation of natural resources are causing irreversible harm to the environment. We must take responsibility for our actions and work towards preserving the environment for the benefit of all living beings.

Practical Ways to Serve Nature

We can serve nature by participating in activities like planting trees, reducing waste, conserving water, and supporting environmentally friendly policies. Such activities affirm the intimate bond between us and nature and promote a sustainable future.

Conclusion

We must serve nature if we wish to maintain a harmonious relationship between humans and the environment. By recognizing our interdependence, taking responsibility for our actions, and engaging in activities to preserve the environment, we can work towards a sustainable future all being on earth-- human and non-human.

***

69. Death

"Transcending the cycle of death and rebirth is the real purpose of this life in human form." —Amma

During one of her Devi Bhava sessions, Amma emphasized the importance of preparing for death, as it is an inevitable part of life. She also mentioned that with the help of scriptures, we can break free from the cycle of birth and death and reach the goal of human life. Many devotees were curious about how to achieve this, and Amma advised them to meditate on the truth of the Self as Brahman.

Devotee 1: Amma, I am afraid of death.

Amma: Fear of death is natural, but we can overcome it by meditating on the truth of the Self. The scriptures teach us that the Self is eternal and infinite, and that it transcends the cycle of birth and death. By reflecting on this truth and meditating on it, we can gradually overcome our fear of death and reach the goal of human life.

Devotee 2: Amma, what is the goal of human life?

Amma: The goal is to realize our true nature as the Self, which is one with Brahman. This realization frees us from the cycle of birth and death and leads to the ultimate goal of moksha, or liberation.

Devotee 3: Amma, can you recommend any specific scriptures or texts that we should study?

Amma: The Upanishads are a great place to start, as they contain the teachings of the sages who have realized the truth of the Self. By studying and reflecting on their teachings, we can gain insight into our true nature and the path to liberation.

Devotee 4: Amma, how do we know when we have achieved the conviction that the Self is free from the cycle of birth and death?

Amma: When we have truly realized the truth of the Self, we will experience a deep inner peace and a sense of freedom that transcends the limitations of the body and mind. This realization is not just intellectual, but experiential, and it transforms our entire being.

Devotee 5: Amma, how can we prepare for death?

Amma: My dear child, death is a natural part of life, and we cannot escape it. However, we can prepare for it by living a life of dharma, by serving others, and by cultivating a spiritual practice. When we live a life of dharma, we create good karma, which helps us to have a peaceful death and a good rebirth.

Devotee 2: Amma, how can we come out of the cycle of birth and death?

Amma: The Upanishads tell us that the Self, which is Brahman, is the essence of our being. When we hear about this Truth and reflect on it, we come to the realization that the Self is free of the cycle of birth and death. We can meditate on this Truth until we have complete conviction in it. Thus, we can transcend the cycle of birth and death.

Commentary
Understanding the Cycle of Death and Rebirth

Amma teaches that the cycle of death and rebirth is a fundamental aspect of the human experience. It is the process by which the soul takes on a new physical form after the death of the body. This cycle is driven by the karmic imprints left by our actions and thoughts in our past lifetimes.

The Importance of Transcending the Cycle

While the cycle of death and rebirth is a natural part of life, Amma teaches that it is not the ultimate goal of human existence. Instead, she encourages us to transcend the cycle by attaining enlightenment, which allows the soul to merge with the divine.

How to Transcend the Cycle

To transcend the cycle of death and rebirth, Amma teaches that one must cultivate spiritual practices such as meditation, selfless service, and devotion to the divine. By purifying the mind and letting go of attachment to the material world, we can begin to experience the true nature of the soul and transcend the cycle of birth and death.

The Ultimate Goal of Transcending the Cycle

The ultimate goal of human life is to find union with the divine and experience eternal peace and bliss. This requires complete surrender of the ego and a deep understanding of the true nature of the self and the universe.

Practical Applications of this Teaching

By focusing on spiritual practices and cultivating detachment from material possessions, we experience a greater sense of peace and contentment. Additionally, the pursuit of enlightenment can motivate us to engage in selfless service and other acts of compassion and kindness, creating a positive impact on the world around us.

Conclusion

Amma's teaching on how to transcend the cycle of death and rebirth encourages us to focus on spiritual practices and to cultivate detachment from material possessions. In this way we can eventually attain enlightenment and escape the cycle of birth and death. This teaching has practical applications in daily life and can motivate individuals to be compassion and kind, here and now.

***

70. Spirituality

"Too much concern about physical security and too little concern about spirituality is the hallmark of today's world."
—Amma

One afternoon a group of youngsters from Amrita Vidyalayam Thrissur approached Amma to ask about cultivating spirituality in a world where money and physical security often take precedence.

Student: Pranams Amma! We are students from Amrita Vidyalayam Thrissur. We have a question for you. You said that too much concern about physical security and too little concern about spirituality is the hallmark of today's world. How can we focus on spirituality when the world is so focused on money and materialism?

Amma: My dear children, it is true that in today's world, many people place a lot of importance on materialistic things like money and physical security. However, it is important to remember that true security comes from within. When we focus on spirituality, we develop a deeper sense of inner peace and contentment. This inner peace can help us face the challenges of life with strength and resilience.

Student: Amma, that makes sense, but how can we focus on spirituality in a world that is so full of distractions and materialism?

Amma: One way is to make spirituality a priority in your life. You can start by setting aside some time each day for reflection, prayer, and meditation. You can also try to surround yourself with people who share your spiritual values and beliefs. Reading spiritual texts, participating in spiritual practices and engaging in selfless service can also help you deepen your spiritual connection.

Student: Thank you, Amma! We will try our best to be as spiritual as possible in our daily lives.

Amma: Remember, my dear children, spirituality is not just about what you do, but also about how you live your life. If you can live with kindness, compassion, and love, you will naturally develop a deeper sense of spirituality.

Commentary
The Culture of Materialism and its Impact
In today's world, people are often driven first and foremost by the pursuit of material success and achievements. This focus on external achievements has led to a lack of attention to spiritual and personal growth. The constant pursuit of material possessions often leaves people feeling empty and unfulfilled, leading to a sense of despair and disillusionment.

The Significance of Spirituality
Amma, however, teaches that true happiness and fulfillment can only be found through spiritual growth and inner development. Through spiritual practice, we can learn to connect with our inner self and find peace and contentment. Spiritual growth helps us to develop virtues such as compassion, love, and kindness, which lead to a deep sense of fulfillment.

Finding Balance in Life
While material success is important, it should not come at the cost of spiritual growth. This is why Amma encourages people to find a balance between material pursuits and spiritual growth. By embracing spirituality, individuals can gain a deeper understanding of themselves and the world around them.

Conclusion
Amma's words remind us that if we wish to lead truly fulfilling lives, we must learn to focus on both material and spiritual pursuits. While material success is important, it should not come at the cost of our spiritual growth.

71. Creation

"There are no mistakes in God's creation. Every creature and every object that has been created by God is so utterly special." – Amma

Amma, was sitting in a serene hut surrounded by nature's beauty. The ocean air was filled with the sweet fragrance of flowers and the happy chirping of birds. Cows grazed nearby, and squirrels frolicked on the nearby tree branches. In the midst of this serene scene, some sadhus from Rishikesh came to seek Amma's guidance. With humility, they prostrated before Amma and asked their questions one by one, eager to imbibe her wisdom.

Amma: My children, it's wonderful to see you all here amidst the beautiful creation of God. The birds, the flowers, the cows, and the squirrels - all of them are God's beautiful creation. What questions do you have for me today?

Sadhu 1: Amma, I have always wondered why God created suffering in this world. Can you please enlighten me on this?

Amma: God did not create suffering, my son. Suffering comes as a result of our own actions. It is there to remind us to realign ourselves with God when we have gone astray from our true nature. It is an opportunity for us to learn and grow and find peace and happiness.

Sadhu 2: Amma, I struggle with controlling my mind during meditation. How can I improve?

Amma: The mind is naturally restless, my son, but with practice and perseverance, it can be trained to be still. Try to meditate regularly and focus on your breath. When your mind wanders, gently bring your attention back to your breath. Over time, the mind will become calmer and more focused.

Sadhu 3: I have been practicing spiritual discipline for many years, Amma, but I feel stuck in my progress. What should I do?

Amma: Progress on the spiritual path can be slow and gradual, but it is important to continue with dedication and faith. Sometimes, our progress is hindered by our own attachments and ego. Try to surrender these to God and focus on serving others selflessly. This will help to purify the mind and accelerate your spiritual growth.

Sadhu 4: Amma. I often feel disconnected from God and struggle with lack of faith. How can I cultivate a stronger connection with God?

Amma: Son, cultivating a strong connection with God requires sincerity and devotion. Practice prayer, meditation, and service with a pure heart and with the intention of connecting with God. Keep an open mind and heart and be receptive to the signs and messages that God may send you. With time and practice, your connection with God will deepen and will become stronger.

Sadhu 5: Amma, I have always wondered about the purpose of God's creation. Why did He create all of this?

Amma: My dear sadhu, God's creation is perfect and beautiful in every way. Every creature, every object has a unique purpose and contributes to the balance of the universe. It is up to us to recognize the beauty of God's creation and to learn from it.

Sadhu 6: But what about the suffering and pain that we see in the world? How does that fit into God's perfect creation, Amma?

Amma: Son, it is true that there is suffering in the world, but it is important to understand that it is a result of our own actions and choices. God's creation is perfect. At the same time, we have free will, and we must take responsibility for the consequences of our actions.

Sadhu 7: Amma, I often wonder why God created different religions and beliefs. Isn't this the cause of most conflicts and wars?

Amma: All religions and beliefs are different paths to the same ultimate goal - to realize God. We must respect and honor each other's beliefs and work together for the greater good. My dear Saddhu, it is only when we let go of our ego and differences that we can truly understand the beauty and perfection of God's creation.

Sadhu 8: Amma, I have always wondered about the role of humans in God's creation. How can we contribute to God's creation?

Amma: My dear sadhu, humans have a great responsibility to take care of God's creation. We must treat every creature and every object with respect and love. We must strive to live in harmony with nature and work towards a better future for all. It is only then that we can truly appreciate the perfection of God's creation.

Sadhu 9: Amma, how can we find God in His creation?

Amma: God is present in every atom of His creation, my son. We must learn to see Him in every creature and every object. It is only then that we can truly appreciate the perfection and beauty of God's creation. Let us all work towards this goal and make the world a better place.

Commentary

In Amma's view, there are no mistakes in God's creation; each creature and object has a unique purpose and value.

Every Creature is Unique

Every creature created by God is special and has a unique purpose. Thus, Amma encourages us treat every living being with love and respect.

Value all of God's Creations

We should appreciate and value all of God's creation, from the tiniest insects to the largest animals. This means becoming conscious of how our actions may impact the environment and the creatures living in it.

Embrace Diversity

Amma says there are no mistakes in God's creation, which implies that we should embrace diversity in all its forms. We must learn to respect all varieties of life, thought, culture, and religion.

Conclusion

Amma conversation with the sadhus serves as a powerful reminder to value and appreciate all of God's creation. It invites us to treat all living beings with respect and to be mindful of our impact on the environment. Ironically, it is by embracing diversity that we find unity and connection with the divine.

***

72. Faith

"Beauty lies in faith, and faith dwells in the heart. Intellect or reasoning is necessary, but we should not let it swallow up the faith within us. We should not allow the intellect to eat up our heart." – Amma

A worried devotee approached Amma seeking guidance about her physical beauty. Amma consoled her and explained that true beauty lies in the beauty of the soul, or Atma.

Amma: Daughter, what's troubling you?

Devotee: Amma, I'm worried about my beauty. I feel like I'm not pretty enough.

Amma: My child, beauty is not just about physical appearance. Beauty lies in faith, and faith dwells in the heart. We must have faith in the divine and in ourselves.

Devotee: But Amma, I still feel like I'm not beautiful enough. What can I do?

Amma: Remember, "Satyam, Shivam, Sundaram" – truth, goodness, and beauty are intertwined. If we have faith in the truth, goodness, and beauty of the Divine, it will reflect in our own beauty. Everything in this world is unique and beautiful in its own way because everything is an image of God. We must strive to see the beauty in everything and everyone, including ourselves.

Amma smiled and held the devotee's hand.

Amma; My dear daughter, you are worried about your external beauty, but true beauty lies within. It is the beauty of the soul, the beauty of the Atma. Your true essence is divine and radiant and that is what makes you truly beautiful.

The devotee looked at Amma with a mix of wonder and confusion.

Devotee: But Amma, how can I find that beauty within myself?

Amma: It is through faith, my child, faith in yourself and faith in the Divine. When we have faith, we can see the beauty in everything around us and that beauty reflects back to us. We should not let our intellect or reasoning override our faith and our heart, for that is where true beauty resides.

Devotee: Amma. I will try to remember this and to have faith in myself.

A sense of peace washed over the devotee. She realized that she had been searching for beauty in all the wrong places, when all along it had been within her.

Commentary
The Importance of Faith

Amma teaches that faith is essential if we wish to live happy lives. Faith gives meaning to our existence and our actions. It provides us with the strength to face challenges and overcome obstacles. Amma says that faith is the foundation of all spiritual and humanitarian work.

The Role of Intellect

At the same time, Amma acknowledges the importance of the intellect and reasoning. She recognizes that it is necessary to use our intelligence to navigate the complexities of life, but we must be careful not to let the intellect overshadow our faith.

Balancing Faith and Intellect

Amma advocates the middle path, where faith and intellect work together in harmony. She believes that those with strong faith can use their intellect to serve humanity. At the same time, those with strong intellects can use their abilities to serve the world, thus deepening their faith and spiritual roots.

Amma's Teachings on Faith and Intellect

Amma's teachings encourage people to cultivate faith while using their intellect to serve others. She emphasizes the importance of having a humble attitude towards faith and being open to learning and growing. By balancing faith and intellect, Amma believes that individuals can lead a fulfilling life while positively impacting the world around them.

Conclusion

Amma's teachings on faith and intellect highlight the importance of finding a balance between the two. By having faith, individuals can find purpose and meaning in life, while using their intellect to serve. By practicing humility and being open to growth, individuals can deepen their faith and contribute to a more compassionate world.

***

73. Stillness

"God is in the present moment. The mind attains a state of stillness when it rests in the present moment. That is where perfect peace and bliss are to be found." – Amma

Amma was approached by a group of brahmacharis who were seeking guidance on how to live in the present moment. Amma's response was simple and enlightening.

Brahmachari 1: Amma, I find it very difficult to be in the present moment. My mind keeps wandering, and I end up worrying about the future or ruminating about the past. How can I overcome this?

Amma: It is natural for the mind to wander, but you need to bring your focus back to the present moment. Whenever you catch your mind wandering, gently remind yourself to be 'now'. This will bring you back to the present and help you experience the stillness and peace that comes with it.

Brahmachari 2: Amma, I feel like I am always rushing through life. How can I slow down and be more present?

Amma: The present moment is the only moment that truly exists. So, slow down and enjoy every moment. When you find yourself rushing, take a deep breath and remind yourself to be 'here'. This will help you appreciate the beauty of the present moment.

Brahmachari 3: Amma, I often find myself getting distracted by external stimuli. How can I stay focused on the present moment?

Amma: The key is to cultivate awareness. When you are fully aware, you will notice the distractions, but they will not take you away from the present moment. So, focus on being 'now' and bring your attention back to the present whenever you get distracted.

Brahmachari 4: Amma, I feel like I am missing out on life because I am always worried about the future. How can I be more present and enjoy the present moment?

Amma: The future is uncertain, and worrying about it will not change anything. The only moment you have is the present moment, so cherish it. When you catch yourself worrying about the future, remind yourself to be 'here' and focus on the present. This will help you experience the joy and beauty of life.

Commentary

Amma encourages us to still our minds and to find perfect peace and bliss in the present moment.

The Importance of Being Present

Rather than being preoccupied with the past or future, Amma invites us to live in the joy of the present moment. By being present, we can fully experience the beauty of life and the beauty of our inner selves.

Attaining Stillness of Mind

The mind can be a constant source of distraction, but Amma teaches us to shift our attention back to the present moment where pure stillness abides. Through meditation and other mindfulness practices, we can quiet the mind and cultivate inner peace.

Finding Perfect Peace and Bliss

By being present and cultivating stillness of mind, we can experience a sense of perfect peace and bliss. This inner state of contentment and joy is not dependent on external circumstances. It is found within each one of us.

Connecting with God in the Present Moment

Amma believes that by connecting with the present moment and finding stillness of mind, we can connect with God. She emphasizes that God is always in the present moment. By being fully present, we can experience this divine connection with Him.

Conclusion
By being present and finding stillness of mind, we can attain inner peace, connection with ourselves, and connection with God. By living in the present moment, we come to know the perfect peace and bliss that is not dependent on external circumstances.

***

74. God

"God is not a limited individual who sits alone up in the clouds on a golden throne. God is the pure Consciousness that dwells within everything. Understanding this truth, learn to accept and love everyone equally." —Amma

One balmy afternoon as the heat of the sun was just beginning to soften, a group of seekers from the Himalayas approached Amma.

Amma: My children, the Truth you seek is already within you. You just need to realize it. The key to unlocking this realization is understanding that God is not a limited individual sitting on a golden throne in the clouds. God is the pure Consciousness that dwells within everything and everyone.

Seeker 1: But Amma, we have been meditating for years and still haven't found this Truth.

Amma: Meditation is important, but spirituality is not just about sitting still and quieting the mind. It's about understanding the nature of the mind and recognizing that the true Self is beyond the mind. Keep meditating, but also try to practice selfless service and love for all beings.

Seeker 2: Amma, how can we love everyone equally? It's not easy.

Amma: It may not be easy, but it is possible. Practice empathy and try to put yourself in other people's shoes. Remember that every person is a manifestation of the same divine Consciousness that dwells within you. Treat everyone with kindness and respect, regardless of their background or beliefs.

Seeker 3: Amma, what about those who have committed heinous crimes? Should we still love them equally?

Amma: Yes, even those who have committed terrible acts are deserving of love and compassion. Remember that they too are manifestations of the same divine Consciousness. This doesn't mean we condone their actions, but we can still strive to see the divine in them and offer them forgiveness and understanding.

Commentary
Amma teaches that God is the pure consciousness that abides everywhere, so we must learn to accept and love everyone equally.

The Nature of God
God is not a limited individual who sits on a golden throne, but rather, the pure consciousness that dwells within everything. Amma teaches that the divine is present in all things and that we can connect with this all-pervasive divinity through spiritual practices.

Pure Consciousness
Pure consciousness is the state of being beyond the mind and thoughts. It is the source of all creation; everything in the universe is an expression of this pure consciousness.

Loving Everyone Equally
Amma exhorts us to accept and love everyone equally. She teaches that because God resides in everything, it is our duty to treat every person and every living being with love and respect. By doing so, we connect with the divine within ourselves and others.

The Benefits of Loving
Loving everyone equally has endless benefits, as it fosters harmony, reduces conflict and creates inclusive and compassionate societies. Additionally, it helps us to connect with the divine within all, leading to spiritual growth and understanding.

Conclusion
Amma believes that if we understand the true nature of God, we will naturally accept and love everyone equally. She encourages us to look beyond the surface and to connect with the divine

consciousness that resides in everything. By doing so, we can create a peaceful and harmonious world.

***

75. God

"God is not confined to a temple or to any specific place. The Divine is omnipresent, omnipotent and can assume any form. Try to behold your Beloved Deity in everything." – Amma

As Amma was talking to some temple priests from Tirumala Temple in Andhra Pradesh, Amma encouraged them to see the Divine in everything and to engage in selfless activities.

Priest: Amma, we are dedicated to serving the Lord in our temple. We have been raised to believe that God is present only here, and we try to maintain the purity of the temple through our rituals and offerings. How can we expand our vision to see God everywhere?

Amma: My dear children, God is not confined to a temple or to any place. The Divine is omnipresent and can assume any form. The trees, the animals, the rivers, the mountains, and even the people around you are all embodiments of God. You can feel the Divine presence everywhere if you look with the right perspective.

Priest: But Amma, how can we be sure that we are serving the Divine and not just performing meaningless rituals?

Amma: The purity of your intentions and actions will determine whether you are serving the Divine or not. Selfless service, compassion, and love are the hallmarks of true devotion. When you serve others with a pure heart, you are serving the Divine in them. When you see everyone as a manifestation of God, you will serve them with humility and love.

Priest: Thank you, Amma. We will try to open our hearts and to serve with love and compassion, seeing God in everyone.

Amma: That is the way to true devotion, my dear children. May the Divine bless you with wisdom and grace on your spiritual journey.

Commentary

Amma teaches that God is omnipresent and encourages us to see the Divine in everything.

God is Not Confined to a Specific Place or Form

Amma reminds us that God is not limited to any specific place. We cannot confine the Divine to a specific location or form because God is present in everything around us. We must learn to recognize the Divine presence in all things.

The Omnipresence of God

We can find the Divine in the vastness of the universe and in the tiniest particles of matter. We do not have to go searching for God in far-off places, for the Divine is always present with us.

Beholding the Divine in Everything

Amma encourages us to see the Divine in everything around us—in the beauty and wonder of the natural world and in the goodness and kindness of others. When we behold the Divine in everything, reverence and gratitude begin to awaken from within.

Omnipresence in Our Daily Lives

By recognizing the omnipresence of God, we can cultivate a sense of connection to the world around us. This helps us to appreciate the beauty and goodness of life, even in difficult times. It also inspires us to treat others with kindness and compassion, for God abides within each person we encounter.

Conclusion

Amma view of God's omnipresence encourages us to look beyond our limited conceptions and to recognize the presence of the Divine in all things. By cultivating this awareness, we can learn to appreciate the beauty and goodness of the world around us and treat others with kindness and compassion.

Dialogues with Amma

***

76. God

"God is not far away from us. It is who we really are, but we need faith to imbibe this truth." – Amma

Amma was sitting on the beach surrounded by a group of Western kids. They were curious about spirituality and had many questions for Amma.

Child 1: Amma, what God is?

Amma: God is not far away from us, my child. God is who we really are. We just need faith to imbibe this truth.

Child 2: But how can we find God within us?

Amma: God resides within us as the Atma, the Self. It is the same in all beings. If we can realize this truth, we will be able to see God in all things.

Child 3: But how can we have faith in something that we cannot see?

Amma: Faith is not just about believing in something that we cannot see. It is about experiencing it in our hearts. When we have faith, we will be able to feel the presence of God within us.

Child 4: Is God only present in temples?

Amma: No, my dear. God is not confined to a temple or to any other holy place. God is omnipresent and can assume any form. We just need to open our hearts and try to behold the Divine in everything around us.

Child 5: How can we make this faith grow in us?

Amma: By practicing selfless service and by meditating regularly. When we serve others without any expectation, we will be able to experience the divinity within them. And when we meditate, we can connect with our inner self and realize the truth of who we really are.

The children listened intently to Amma's words and felt a sense of peace and calmness arise in their hearts. In that moment, they realized that spirituality was something that they could experience within themselves.

Commentary
The Proximity of God
Amma does not believe that God is something far away and inaccessible. Instead, God is ever-present and dwells within everything. In reality, we are never separate from God; we are intimately connected with the Divine at all times.

The Importance of Faith
Despite the omnipresence of God, it is important to develop faith to understand and connect with the Divine. Faith allows us to trust in something beyond ourselves and to open ourselves up to the mysteries of the universe.

Understanding the True Nature of God
To understand the true nature of God, Amma suggests that we look beyond conventional ideas and dogma. Rather than thinking of God as something specific, she encourages us to view God as a state of consciousness that is accessible to all.

Embodying the Divine
Amma teaches that in order to truly connect with God, we need to embody the Divine in our thoughts, words, and actions. Living a life of love, compassion, and service to others is what awakens us to the divinity in everyone and everything around us.

Conclusion
Amma says that we must develop faith in order to understand the true nature of God. She teaches that God is not something far away, but rather, ever-present within us and in the world around us. By embodying the Divine in acts of love, compassion and service, we eventually become one with the Divine.

77. Guru

"The scriptures and the great Masters remind us that the Self, or God, is our true nature." — Amma

Once as Amma was speaking with a group of monks from the Ramakrishna Mission in Cochin, the monks expressed a keen desire to know more about the nature of the Self and how to realize it. The monks posed insightful questions and listened intently as Amma responded.

Monk 1: Amma, you said that the Self is our true nature. How can we realize this truth?

Amma: Through meditation and self-inquiry, we can gradually purify our minds and come to know the Self. The scriptures and the teachings of the great Masters can guide us in this process.

Monk 2: Amma, can you give us some practical tips on how to practice meditation and self-inquiry?

Amma: Of course, son. To begin with, find a quiet place, where you can sit comfortably and undisturbed for some time. Close your eyes and focus your attention on your breath. Watch the breath as it goes in and out. Whenever your mind gets distracted, gently bring it back to the breath. This is a simple but powerful technique that can help you develop concentration and inner peace. As for self-inquiry, you can start by asking yourself the question "Who am I?" and exploring the nature of your true identity.

Monk 3: Amma, what role do the scriptures play in our spiritual journey?

Amma: The scriptures are like a road-map that can guide us towards our destination. They contain the teachings of the great Masters who have realized the truth and can show us the way. By studying and contemplating the scriptures, we can gain a deeper understanding into our true nature and into the path to realization.

Monk 4: Amma, what are some common obstacles that we might encounter on the spiritual path?

Amma: There are many obstacles on the spiritual path, such as attachment to worldly pleasures, ego, ignorance, and lack of faith. But with perseverance, humility, and surrender to the Divine, we can overcome these obstacles and progress towards the goal. Remember that the Divine is always with us, guiding and supporting us. Always remember that we are never alone.

Commentary
The Self and God Are One

Amma confirms that the true nature of every individual is the Self, God. Each one of us is a divine being, and our ultimate goal in life is to realize this truth and merge with the divinity within. We can achieve this through spiritual practices such as meditation, selfless service, and devotion to God.

The Role of Scriptures and Spiritual Teachers

Amma often points to the scriptures and the guidance of spiritual teachers as the key to realizing our true nature. Guided by their wisdom, we can navigate the challenges of life and deepen our understanding of the Self.

Realizing Our True Nature Through Self-Awareness

Amma teaches that self-awareness is essential in realizing our true nature. By turning our attention inward and observing our thoughts, emotions, and actions, we can begin to understand the nature of the mind and the true nature of the Self. Through spiritual practices such as meditation and selfless service, we can cultivate self-awareness and develop a deeper connection with the Divine.

Living a Life of Love and Service

Amma embodies love and service to others. Through her words and example, she teaches us to serve others with compassion and kindness. In this way, we purify our hearts and minds and develop qualities such as humility, gratitude, and empathy. When we develop these qualities, a deep connection with the divine springs up from within.

Conclusion

Amma's teachings offer a holistic approach to spirituality, emphasizing the importance of self-awareness, compassion, and service to others. By realizing our true nature as divine beings, and by living a life of love and service, we can experience divine peace, joy, and fulfillment.

***

78. Love

"Our duty towards God is compassion and love towards the poor and needy." – Amma

Amma's ashram provides food to all the villagers who come without any distinction. Once, some years ago, one of the brahmachari questioned this practice.

Brahmachari: Amma, I have a question. What is the use of giving food to everyone who comes to the ashram, without any distinction? There are some people who are wealthy and can afford to buy food, while there are others who are poor and truly need it. Shouldn't we focus on helping the poor and needy, rather than just giving food to anyone who comes?

Amma: My dear child, compassion and love towards the poor and needy is our duty towards God. But who are the poor and needy? Is it just those who don't have money to buy food? Or is it also those who are hungry for love and affection, those who are hungry for spiritual guidance and support?

Brahmachari: I had not thought of that, Amma. But still, wouldn't it be better to focus on helping those who are truly in need?

Amma: Every person who comes to the ashram is in need, my child. Some may not show it on the outside, but on the inside, they are suffering. Maybe they are lonely, maybe they are searching for something that they can't find in the outside world. By giving them food and welcoming them into our ashram, we are showing them that they are not alone, that there are people who care about them.

Brahmachari: Thank you for helping me to see.

Amma: Always remember, son, that compassion and love are the most powerful tools we have in this world. By using them, we can transform our lives and the lives of others as well.

Commentary
Compassion for Those in Need

Amma believes that serving those in need is one of the most important ways to serve God. She encourages people to show compassion towards the less fortunate and to actively work towards improving their lives.

Love as Worship

Love is a powerful force that can bring us closer to God. Amma says that we can show our devotion to God through acts of love and kindness towards all beings.

Selfless Service

Amma teaches that selfless service is a path to spiritual growth and enlightenment. By serving others, without expecting anything in return, we can purify our minds and hearts and become more attuned to the Divine.

Conclusion

It is our duty towards God to develop the qualities of compassion, love, and selfless service in our spiritual journey. When we serve others, a deep sense of meaning, purpose and connection with the Divine enters in our lives.

***

79. Wealth

"While many enjoy partying and throwing away their wealth, many others can't even afford a single meal a day."

—Amma

A group of wealthy devotees from the United States recently came to speak with Amma about how to use their wealth to benefit others. Recognizing the disparity between the wealthy and the poor, these devotees were trying to find ways to make a positive impact and help those in need.

Amma: Welcome, my children. It's a pleasure to have you here. I understand that you have come with a question. Please feel free to ask me anything.

Devotee 1: Thank you, Amma. We are blessed to have the resources that we do, and we want to use them to help others. But sometimes it's hard to know where to start. How can we make the biggest impact?

Amma: The first step is to realize that there are many people in this world who are struggling to survive. While some have the luxury of partying and throwing away their wealth, many others can't obtain even a single meal a day. So, the best way to use your wealth is to help people like them. There are many organizations and charities that work towards providing basic necessities like food, shelter, and healthcare to the poor. I would suggest finding a cause that resonates with you and to support it through donations and volunteer work.

Devotee 2: That's a great suggestion, Amma. But how can we be sure that our money is being used effectively? There are so many charities out there, and it's hard to know which ones are actually making a difference.

Amma: That is a valid concern, my child. It's important to do your research before donating to any organization. Look for charities that have a proven track record of making a positive impact, and ones that are transparent about how they use their funds. You can also reach out to charities directly and ask about their programs and the people they serve. By doing your homework, you can ensure that your money is being used in the most effective way possible.

Devotee 3: Amma, what about giving directly to people in need? Is that a good way to help?

Amma: Giving directly to people in need can certainly be a powerful way to help, my child. However, it's important to do so in a way that is respectful and dignified. Instead of just handing out money or gifts, take the time to talk to the people you are trying to help, and understand their needs and challenges. Offer your support in a way that empowers them and helps them build a better future for themselves and their families.

Devotee 4: Thank you, Amma. Your guidance is invaluable. We will do our best to use our wealth to serve.

Amma: Remember, my children, that the true measure of wealth is not in what we accumulate, but in what we give back to the world. May your actions be guided by love and compassion, and may you make a positive impact on the lives of others.

Commentary

In this conversation with her wealthy devotees, Amma stresses the importance of showing love and compassion towards those who are less fortunate.

The Disparity Wealth

Amma invites us to contemplate the stark contrast between those who have the means to enjoy life's luxuries and those who struggle to meet their basic needs. This disparity is a reality in many parts of the world, where poverty and hunger continue to be major issues.

Our Responsibility as Human Beings

As human beings, it is our responsibility to uplift those who are going through hard times. We have a duty to help those who are less fortunate and to show compassion towards them. This is not just a moral imperative, but a spiritual one as well.

The Importance of Compassion and Love

Compassion and love are essential in our interactions with others, particularly with those who are struggling. Amma teaches that when we show love and compassion, we are not only helping others but also ourselves. When we love and serve, joy and fulfillment bless our lives.

Service as Spiritual Practice

Service to others is a central theme in Amma's teachings. She emphasizes that serving others is not just a way to help those in need but also a means to achieve spiritual growth. By helping others, we learn to put aside our own ego and desires and to focus on the needs of others.

Amma's Legacy of Service

Amma's teachings on compassion and service have inspired countless individuals around the world to engage in acts of kindness and service to others. Her organization, Embracing the World, runs numerous charitable initiatives to help those in need providing disaster relief, healthcare, and education.

Conclusion

Amma words of compassion and love remind us of our duty towards our poor and needy brothers and sisters. Through acts of service and compassion, we bring spiritual and emotional upliftment to the world and to ourselves.

***

80. God

"We should always maintain the awareness and understanding that no matter what we do, the power behind our actions is God's. Offering your own self into the burning yajna kunda of the infinite power that is God—that is real seva. Atma-samarpanam—offering yourself—is a law of the universe. A few rare individuals live according to this truth. Most are ignorant of it altogether." —Amma

A group of scholars and practitioners of Vedanta once came to visit Amma at her ashram, seeking her guidance on spiritual matters. These seekers hailed from the esteemed Shankara Veda Shala and were well-versed in the sacred texts and practices of the Vedic tradition.

Amma, welcomed the group with open arms, eager to discuss spirituality with them. One of the central themes of their conversation was the ancient Sanskrit phrase, "Vasudhaiva Kutumbakam," which means, "The whole world is one family." Throughout their discussion, Amma and the Vedic group explored the meaning and significance of this phrase and explored how it can guide our actions and relationships with others.

Amma: Welcome, my dear children. I understand you are visiting from Shankara Veda Shala. It's wonderful to have you here at our ashram.

Vedic Scholar 1: Thank you, Amma. We have come to seek your guidance on how to better serve the Divine through our actions. We have been studying the Vedas and performing yajnas, but we want to deepen our understanding of the spiritual principles behind them.

Amma: That's a noble goal, my child. It's important to remember that all of our actions should be done with the awareness that the power behind them is God's. This understanding can transform even the simplest of tasks into a form of seva.

Vedic Scholar 2: Amma, can you give us an example of how we can offer ourselves into the infinite power of God?

Amma: Of course, my child. One way to do this is through atma-samarpanam, offering yourself to God. This is a law of the universe, but only a few rare individuals live according to this truth. By offering ourselves into the burning yajna kunda of the infinite power that is God, we can truly serve the divine.

Vedic Scholar 3: Amma, we have been taught about the concept of Vasudhaiva Kutumbakam, that the whole world is one family. Can you speak more about this?

Amma: Vasudhaiva Kutumbakam is a beautiful concept from the ancient scriptures of India. It recognizes that all of us are part of the same human family, and that we should treat each other with love and compassion. By serving others and recognizing their inherent divinity, we can deepen our own spiritual understanding and connection to God.

Vedic Scholar 4: Thank you, Amma. We will continue on the path of seva.

Amma: Always remember that the power behind our actions is God's, my children. By serving others with love and compassion, we can truly offer ourselves to the divine. May we all work towards the realization of Vasudhaiva Kutumbakam, and may we treat all beings as members of our own family.

Commentary
The Power behind our Actions
Amma explains that God is the source of all power and that everything we do is powered by God.

Self-Offering
Amma describes the concept of Atma-samarpanam, or offering of oneself to God, as a law of the universe.

Rare Individuals

Amma acknowledges that few people live according to this truth; nonetheless, it is an essential aspect of spiritual growth.

God's Presence

Amma's teachings emphasize the importance of recognizing God's presence in all aspects of our life and dedicating ourselves to serving others. By understanding that God is the source of all power, we can approach our actions with humility and gratitude.

Surrendering to the Divine

One of the most important things we can do is to surrender our individual selves to the larger power of God. This means recognizing that everything we do is an expression of the Divine.

Atma-samarpanam

The act of surrendering oneself to God is known as Atma-samarpanam. This requires a deep level of faith and trust in the power of the Divine. Inspired by this truth, rare individuals offer themselves in service to others and the Divine. Amma's teachings encourage us to cultivate this noble truth in our daily lives by working selflessly for others. Thus, Amma highlights the importance of surrendering ourselves to God, recognizing that all actions are ultimately performed through the power of the Divine.

Conclusion

By surrendering ourselves to the Divine, we align ourselves with a larger purpose and find a vastly deeper sense of peace and contentment.

***

81. Feelings

"The feelings 'I am superior' and 'I am inferior' are both products of the ego." –Amma

In this dialogue, Amma speaks with the brahmacharis and householders about how to recognize and overcome the ego's sneaky ways.

Amma: Today, I would like to talk to you about how the illusion of the ego can sneak into our thoughts and feelings. We often believe that we are either superior or inferior to others, but both of these feelings are products of the ego. Such feelings create division and conflict within us and others. So, let us be mindful and careful of this illusion. Who would like to share their thoughts on this topic?

Brahmachari 1: Amma, I have noticed that sometimes I feel superior to others because of my spiritual practice and knowledge. I know this is wrong, but it's hard to shake off this feeling.

Amma: Yes, my child. It's easy to fall into the trap of believing that we are somehow better than others. But remember, the true essence of spirituality is humility and compassion. We should use our knowledge to serve others and uplift them, not to elevate ourselves above them. Keep this in mind and stay mindful of the ego's sneaky ways.

Householder 1: Amma, I struggle with feelings of inferiority. I often compare myself with others and feel like I'm not good enough.

Amma: I understand, my child. This feeling of inferiority can also be a product of the ego. Remember that each of us has our unique talents and strengths, and we should celebrate and use them to serve others. Instead of comparing ourselves with others, let us focus on our own growth and evolution as spiritual beings. We are all valuable and worthy of love and respect, regardless of our perceived shortcomings or flaws.

Brahmachari 2: Amma, I sometimes feel both superior and inferior at the same time, like I'm better than some people but not as good as others.

Amma: That is a common experience, my son. The ego can create a lot of confusion and contradictory feelings within us. The key is to recognize these feelings as products of the ego and to detach from them. Remember that we are all divine beings, equal in the eyes of God. Let us focus on cultivating love and compassion towards all and let go of these illusory feelings of superiority or inferiority.

Householder 2: Amma, what can we do to overcome ego-driven feelings and thoughts?

Amma: The first step is to recognize and acknowledge them. When we become aware of such thoughts and feelings, we can begin to detach from them and see them for what they truly are. We can also practice mindfulness and meditation to quiet the ego's voice and connect with our true divine nature. Ultimately, it is through selfless service and devotion to God that we can transcend the ego and experience true unity with all beings.

Commentary
The Ego and Self-Perception
The ego is often responsible for creating a distorted self-perception, leading to a sense of superiority or inferiority, both of which can hinder our spiritual growth and diminish our inner peace.

The Illusion of Superiority
When we feel superior to others, we may become arrogant, judgmental, and condescending. This can create a sense of separation from others and block the ability to empathize and connect with them.

The Illusion of Inferiority
When we feel inferior to others, we may become self-doubting, insecure, and lack confidence. This can lead to negative self-talk and a lack of self-love and self-acceptance.

Overcoming the Ego
Overcoming the ego requires self-awareness and a willingness to let go of the need for external validation. By recognizing that we are all interconnected and equal in our humanity, we can cultivate humility and a deeper sense of compassion towards ourselves and others.

Conclusion
Amma's words remind us that the ego can create false self-perception that can hinder our growth and well-being. By recognizing the illusions of superiority and inferiority, we can work towards overcoming the ego and cultivate a deeper sense of connection and compassion towards ourselves and others.

***

82. Master

"The master destroys obstacles and reveals the sacred path to the seeker." –Amma

The Kali temple was adorned with beautiful decorations, as the soothing sounds of Swami Amritageetananda's bhajans filled the hall. As Amma lovingly greeted each person, a seeker from Ranchi approached her with a plea for guidance. He was facing many obstacles in his life. Amma, the ever-compassionate guide, offered words of wisdom and encouragement to help him navigate his path forward.

Seeker: Amma, I have been struggling with so many obstacles. How can I overcome them?

Amma: My dear child, obstacles are a natural part of life. It is how we approach them that determines their impact on our journey. Remember that obstacles can be teachers, guiding us to deepen our understanding and strengthen our resolve. When we surrender to the divine will, and trust in the master's guidance, the path will reveal itself.

Seeker: But how can I trust the master's guidance? How do I know which path to follow?

Amma: The master is always present within and around us, guiding us towards our highest good. Through prayer, meditation, and service to others, we can cultivate a deeper connection to the divine and receive guidance from the master. It is important to be open and receptive to the signs and messages that come our way, and to have faith that the master will reveal the path to us when we are ready.

Seeker: Thank you, Amma.

Amma: Remember, the master is always with you, supporting and guiding you on your journey. Surrender to the divine will, my child, and obstacles will be transformed into opportunities for transformation.

Commentary
The Role of a Spiritual Master

Amma consistently emphasizes the importance of a having a spiritual master on the path. The spiritual master not only removes obstacles, but also provides needed guidance. This helps seekers to deepen their spiritual practice and to overcome the limitations of the ego.

The Importance of Obstacles

Obstacles are a natural part of the spiritual journey and serve as opportunities for growth and self-discovery. Amma encourages seekers to view obstacles as challenges that can help them develop spiritual strength and resilience.

The Sacred Path

Amma teaches that the path to self-realization is a sacred journey that requires dedication, perseverance, and faith. She also emphasizes the importance of cultivating spiritual qualities such as love, compassion, and humility as one travels along the path.

Conclusion

Seeking guidance and support on the spiritual journey is crucial. True spiritual masters help seekers to navigate obstacles and lead them to their true path in life. By embracing the challenges and opportunities presented by the journey, seekers can deepen their spiritual practice and cultivate the qualities necessary for self-realization.

***

83. Love
"Divine Love is our true essence." —Amma

Once a young aspirant from the Iskon community approached Amma with a question about divine love.

Seeker: Amma, I have been trying understand the true essence of divine love. Can you help me understand how to connect with it?

Amma: Divine love is our true essence, dear child. It is the purest expression of the soul, and it is always within us, waiting to be awakened. To connect with it, we must first let go of the illusion of separateness that the ego creates. We must open our hearts to the divine light within, and let it guide us on our path of service and devotion.

Seeker: But Amma, how can we know if we are truly connected to the divine?

Amma: When we are connected to the divine, we feel a deep sense of peace, joy, and love within. We are able to see the divine in all beings and things, and our actions become guided by compassion and the highest truth. So, keep seeking, dear child, and know that the divine love within you will always lead you to where you need to be.

Seeker: Thank you, Amma. I will treasure these words on my journey.

Amma: May the divine love within you continue to blossom and guide you, my son.

Commentary
The Meaning of Divine Love

Amma teaches that divine love is the universal force that connects us all. It is not limited to any particular religion, race, or culture. Divine love is unconditional, selfless, and non-judgmental. It is the essence of our being, and it is the driving force behind all of our actions. This love is not something that can be acquired or earned; rather, it is something that already exists within us.

Embracing Divine Love

Amma emphasizes the importance of embracing divine love because it is the key to experiencing true happiness and inner peace. When we embrace this love, we begin to see the world and others through a different lens. We begin to see the interconnectedness of all beings, and we begin to understand that the well-being of others is just as important as our own.

Cultivating Divine Love

Amma suggests that one of the best ways to cultivate divine love is through selfless service. When we serve others without any expectation of reward or recognition, we begin to experience the joy and fulfillment that comes from giving. Another way to cultivate divine love is through spiritual practices such as meditation, prayer, and chanting.

Experiencing Divine Love

When we experience Divine Love, we begin to see the world in a different way. We begin to experience a sense of inner peace, joy, and contentment that is not dependent on external circumstances. We begin to develop a greater sense of compassion and understanding for others, and we become more connected to the world around us.

Conclusion

Amma's words reminds us of the importance of divine love in our lives. By embracing this love and cultivating it through selfless service and spiritual practices, we experience a sense of inner peace and fulfillment that cannot be found through material possessions or external achievements. Divine love is the key to experiencing true happiness. It is not something we have to search for, it already exists within each and every one of us.

***

84. Parents

"Parents have a great influence on their children. If they are morally good, the children will also be good." – Amma

One day, a young boy and his parents came to see Amma. The parents were seeking guidance about their son who had been neglecting his studies. He was spending most of his time playing. Amma listened patiently to their concerns and offered her insights.

Amma: Your look worried. What's troubling you?

Parent: Our son is not studying; he is always playing. We are worried about his future.

Amma: I see. How old is your son?

Parent: He is fifteen years old.

Amma: Well, as parents, you have a great influence on your child's behavior. Have you talked to him about the importance of education?

Parent: Yes, we have, but he doesn't seem to listen.

Amma: Perhaps you can try to find out why he is not interested in studying. Is he having any difficulties at school?

Parent: No, he is doing well in his studies.

Amma: Then, it could be that he is not finding his studies interesting or challenging enough. You could try to encourage him to pursue his interests and passions and find ways to make his studies more engaging.

Parent: That's a great suggestion, Amma. But what if he still doesn't listen?

Amma: Remember, as parents, it's important to lead by example. If you are morally good and responsible, your child will be influenced by your behavior. Never forget to shower your child with love and affection. That is the most important thing.

Parent: Thank you, Amma. We will try.

Amma: Blessings to you and your family. May your child find his path in life with the guidance of the Divine.

Commentary

In this conversation, Amma emphasizes the important role mothers and fathers play in shaping their children's moral values.

The Power of Parental Influence

Amma often highlights the tremendous influence parents have on their children's upbringing.

The Responsibility of Parents

Amma teaches that parents have a responsibility to set a positive example for their children and to instill moral values in them.

Impact on Society

Amma believes that children who are raised with strong moral values will make positive contributions to society when they become adults.

The Role of Spirituality

Amma emphasizes the importance of spirituality in raising children, as it helps to cultivate love, compassion and selflessness.

Conclusion

Parents play a critical role in shaping their children's moral values. Amma emphasizes that parents must take responsibility for instilling these values and setting a good example. By doing so, children will grow up to make positive contributions to society. Amma also stresses the importance of spirituality, as it helps cultivate essential qualities like love, compassion, and selflessness.

***

85. Mind

"The real mistake humans have committed is their inability to differentiate between requirements and luxuries." —Amma.

During one of her tours in South India, Amma met a family who had built three houses and were facing a financial crisis. The family was in a dilemma as to which house they should sell to alleviate their financial burden. Amma engaged in a dialogue with the family members to help them understand the difference between requirements and luxuries.

Amma: Namaste. I heard that you are planning to sell one of your houses. Can you tell me why you are making this decision?

Family Member 1: Yes, Amma. We have built three houses, and now we are facing a financial crisis. We cannot afford to maintain all three houses, so we have decided to sell one of them.

Amma: I understand. Which one are you planning to sell?

Family Member 2: We are confused, Amma. Each one of us has a different opinion. I want to sell the first house because it has become old, and we need to spend a lot of money on repairs. But my brother wants to sell the third house because it has a bigger garden.

Family Member 3: I think we should sell the second house. It's in a remote area, and it's difficult to find renters.

Amma: I see. But have you thought about what you really need and what is a luxury?

Family Member 1: What do you mean, Amma?

Amma: You own three houses, and yet you are facing a financial crisis. Have you thought about selling all three houses and buying a smaller house that would fulfill your basic needs?

Family Member 2: But Amma, we have worked hard to build these houses. We cannot just sell them like that.

Amma: I understand your attachment to your houses, but you also need to think practically. If you are maintaining three houses, you are living for luxury rather than necessity.

Family Member 3: But Amma, we cannot compromise on our comfort.

Amma: Of course, you should not compromise on your comfort, but you need to differentiate between what is a requirement and what is a luxury. A big garden and a remote area may be luxuries that you can live without.

Family Member 1: So, what should we do, Amma?

Amma: Think about what is essential for your family's well-being and what you can do without. Sell the house that is not a requirement and use the money wisely to secure your future.

Family Member 2: Thank you, Amma. You always show us the right path.

Amma: My blessings are always with you. Remember, simplicity is the key to a peaceful life.

Commentary

In this dialogue, Amma emphasizes the importance of differentiating between requirements and luxuries. Requirements are those essential things that are necessary for survival, such as food, shelter, and clothing. Luxuries, on the other hand, are things that are not necessary for survival but are desired for pleasure or comfort.

Meeting our requirements is crucial. We all need the basic necessities to survive. Without fulfilling these basic needs, it is impossible to sustain ourselves. Amma stresses the importance of fulfilling these requirements before seeking luxuries in life.

While luxuries can add value to life, mistaking them for requirements can have a negative impact on our lives. Materialistic living can lead to a never-ending cycle of wanting more and more, leading to problems such as debt, stress, and discontentment.

Furthermore, neglecting real necessities for the sake of luxuries can lead to dire consequences, such as poor health, financial instability, and emotional turmoil. Therefore, it is essential to recognize and prioritize real necessities over luxuries.

To embrace simplicity, individuals need to cultivate awareness and learn to let go of unnecessary desires. By focusing on real necessities, individuals can experience more contentment and peace in their lives. Living a simple life can also lead to reduced stress, improved mental health, and greater financial stability.

Thus, Amma stresses the importance of recognizing and fulfilling our requirements while being mindful of the impact of mistaking luxuries for necessities. Embracing simplicity and focusing on real necessities can lead to a more contented and peaceful life.

***

86. Gratitude

"We should try to cultivate an attitude of gratitude. That will help us to earn God's grace." – Amma

During one of her tours in North India, Amma stopped for lunch with her ashramites. Before the meal, they all meditated with Amma, and one of the Western devotees took the opportunity to ask Amma about cultivating an attitude of gratitude. The devotee engaged in a lengthy dialogue with Amma, seeking her wisdom on this topic

Western Devotee: Amma, during meditation, I was thinking about gratitude. How can we cultivate an attitude of gratitude?

Amma: Gratitude is essential. It helps us to appreciate the good things we have and makes us content and happy.

Western Devotee: But how can we cultivate it?

Amma: We should start by counting our blessings and being thankful for them. We often take things for granted and don't realize how blessed we are.

Western Devotee: Yes, that's true. But sometimes, it's challenging to be grateful when we are going through tough times.

Amma: That's when gratitude becomes even more critical. We should learn to see the lessons in our hardships and be grateful for the growth opportunities they bring.

Western Devotee: I see. But what about when we are happy and things are going well?

Amma: Even then, we should be grateful. We should recognize that our happiness is not permanent and that we are blessed to experience it at that moment.

Western Devotee: That makes sense, Amma. But sometimes, it's hard to be grateful when we see others suffering.

Amma: That's when compassion comes in. We should use our blessings to help others and be grateful for the opportunity to make a difference in their lives.

Western Devotee: That's a beautiful way to look at it, Amma.

Amma: Remember, my child, an attitude of gratitude is the key to earning God's grace.

Commentary
Cultivating an Attitude of Gratitude
Gratitude is a powerful tool that can transform our lives. Amma encourages us to cultivate an attitude of gratitude by appreciating the blessings in our lives, no matter how small they may be. Amma believes that when we express gratitude, we create positive energy that attracts more blessings into our lives.

The Benefits of Gratitude
Amma teaches that gratitude has several benefits. It helps us to focus on the positive aspects of our lives, which can improve our mental health and well-being. Gratitude also promotes empathy and kindness, which can enhance our relationships with others. In fact, studies have shown that practicing gratitude can improve our physical health and lead to better sleep, increased resilience, and reduced stress levels.

Gratitude and Spirituality
Gratitude is an essential aspect of spiritual practice. Amma teaches that by expressing gratitude, we come to recognize the divine presence in our lives and acknowledge our interconnectedness with all beings. Gratitude can also deepen our faith and trust in the universe, which can bring us closer to God.

Gratitude in Action
Amma encourages us to put our gratitude into action by serving others. She believes that by using our blessings to help others, we express our gratitude in a tangible way. For Amma, service to humanity is the highest form of devotion and the greatest expression of our love for God.

Conclusion

Amma's teachings on gratitude remind us of the importance of appreciating all of the blessings in our lives. By cultivating an attitude of gratitude, we can improve our well-being, enhance our relationships, and deepen our spirituality. Amma encourages us to express our gratitude in action by serving others, which will bring us closer to God and create a brighter world.

***

87. Spirituality

"We live in the age of the Internet. Wherever we go on the planet, we need to have the Internet. But, along with an Internet connection, we also need to rediscover our 'Inner-net' connection. Spirituality teaches us how to manage both our internal and external worlds." – Amma

During a beautiful sunset by the seaside, Amma was approached by a young family seeking guidance on how to balance the use of the internet with their spiritual lives. The father expressed his concerns about his young son spending too much time on his phone and laptop and wondered how to find a healthy balance.

Father: Amma, my son is always on his phone or laptop. I'm worried that he's spending too much time on the internet. How much time should we allow young children to spend on their phones and computers?

Amma: The internet has become an integral part of our lives, but we need to learn to balance our use of it. We should limit the time we spend on the internet and use it wisely.

Father: But how do we find the balance between using the internet and practicing spirituality?

Amma: It's essential to rediscover our 'Inner-net' connection. Spirituality teaches us how to manage both our internal and external worlds. We need to develop mindfulness and discipline and make sure that we don't neglect our spiritual practices.

Father: That's true, but it's challenging to control the internet use of young children. They are always on their phones or laptops.

Amma: As parents, we need to set boundaries and guide our children towards responsible internet use. We should encourage them to spend more time in nature, engage in physical activities, and cultivate their hobbies and interests.

Father: I see. Thank you for your guidance, Amma. You always have a way of putting things into perspective.

Amma: My blessings are with you and your family always. Remember, technology is a tool that should enhance our lives, not control them.

Commentary

Amma emphasizes the need for maintaining a balance between our inner and outer worlds in the age of the Internet. While we depend on the Internet for our daily lives, we also need to cultivate a connection with our inner self.

The Internet's Impact on Our Lives

In today's world, the Internet has become an integral part of our lives. From socializing to shopping, the Internet has revolutionized the way we do things. It has brought people closer, created new job opportunities, and enhanced our access to all kinds of information.

The Importance of Our 'Inner-net'

However, with all these benefits, we may have lost touch with our inner selves. The constant use of social media and other online platforms can lead to a disconnect from our own thoughts and emotions. Amma's term, the 'Inner-net', refers to the connection with our inner, spiritual selves.

The Role of Spirituality in Our Lives

Amma believes that spirituality can help us manage both our internal and external worlds. It teaches us to cultivate a sense of gratitude, compassion, and self-awareness. Spirituality can help us find a sense of purpose and meaning in our lives.

Balancing the Internet and Spirituality

To maintain a healthy balance between the Internet and our spiritual lives, we must learn to disconnect from the online world and reconnect with ourselves. We can do this by practicing mindfulness, meditation, and other spiritual practices. By cultivating a connection with our inner selves, we can enhance our overall well-being and happiness.

Conclusion

While the Internet has many benefits, it is important to remember the value of our 'Inner-net' connection. Spirituality helps us to balance our inner and outer worlds and to cultivate a sense of purpose and meaning in our lives. By taking time to disconnect from the on-line world and reconnect with ourselves, we can enhance our overall well-being and happiness.

***

88. Grace

"Every situation created by the master is a gift of grace, meant to remove the ego." – Amma

During a private room darshan with Amma, a devotee had the opportunity to ask about grace and the destruction of the ego.

Devotee: Amma, can you please explain to me what you mean when you say, "Every situation created by the master is a Gift of grace meant to remove the ego"?

Amma: Every moment of our life is a gift of grace from the Divine. Every situation that we encounter, whether pleasant or unpleasant, is meant to help us grow and evolve spiritually. When we face challenging situations, it helps us to let go of our ego and surrender to the Divine will.

Devotee: That makes sense, Amma. But how do we know if a situation is a gift of grace or just a difficult experience?

Amma: It's all a matter of perspective, my daughter. When we face difficult situations, we have two options: we can either react with anger, frustration, and despair, or we can choose to see the situation as an opportunity for growth and learning. The choice is always ours.

Devotee: I understand, Amma. But how do we remove the ego through these situations?

Amma: When we face difficult situations, it is an invitation to let go of our attachment to our ego and to surrender to the Divine will. It is only through surrendering that we can experience true peace and liberation. So, every situation created by the master is an opportunity to let go of our ego and surrender to the Divine.

Devote: Thank you, Amma. You have given me a lot to reflect on.

Amma: You are always welcome, my daughter. Remember that every moment of your life is a gift of grace, meant to help you evolve and grow spiritually. May the grace of the Divine be with you always

Commentary
The Master's Role in Our Lives

Amma teaches that the Master, or the Divine, plays an essential role in our lives, and she encourages us to see every situation we encounter as a gift of grace. If we can consistently choose this perspective, every event in our lives, whether positive or negative, carries a lesson to be learned.

The Significance of Grace

Grace is an essential aspect of Amma's teachings. She believes that every experience in our lives is a result of the grace of the Divine. When we approach life with this attitude, we learn and grow, and become better versions of ourselves. It is up to us to recognize and appreciate the grace that we receive, even in difficult situations.

The Ego's Impact on Our Lives

Amma teaches that the ego often creates barriers that prevent us from understanding the deeper meaning of our experiences. The ego creates a sense of separation and leads us to believe that we are separate from the Divine. By recognizing and letting go of our ego, we can open ourselves up to a deeper understanding of ourselves and the world around us.

The Importance of Self-Reflection

In order to fully appreciate the lessons we learn from the Master, Amma encourages self-reflection. It is through introspection and contemplation that we can gain a deeper understanding of ourselves and our place in the world. By reflecting on our experiences, we can learn to recognize the Divine in all aspects of life.

89. Amma
"Amma sees everything as part of the whole, as an extension of Her own Self." —Amma

Darshan is the act of seeing or being in the presence of a spiritual teacher or guru. It is considered a sacred experience where the devotee has the opportunity to receive blessings, guidance, and insights from the guru. Once a Swami was blessed to have Amma's darshan and the following conversation took place.

Swami: Amma, how do you see everything around you?

Amma: Swami, I see everything as part of the whole, as an extension of my own Self. I don't perceive any separation between me and the world. It's like the ocean and its waves. The ocean is the whole, and the waves are the individual aspects. But they are all part of the same ocean. In the same way, I see everything as a part of the Divine Consciousness.

Swami: But Amma, how do you manage to maintain this perception in every moment, even in the midst of so many different people and situations?

Amma: Swami, it's a constant practice. I try to remain mindful and present in every moment, and I remind myself that everything and everyone is an extension of my own Self. Through this practice, I am able to maintain this perception and see the world as a manifestation of the Divine.

Swami: Thank you, Amma. Your words are a great inspiration to me.

Amma: May the grace of the Divine be with you, Swami.

Commentary

Amma sees everything in the world as interconnected, as an extension of her own being. She does not see any separation between herself and others. Instead, she sees herself as part of a larger whole.

Interconnectedness

Amma suggests that everything we do and experience is interconnected and affects the whole. As such, we should treat others with love and compassion because they are a part of ourselves. If we can live with this perspective, unity and harmony will blossom in our lives and in the world.

Seeing Everything as Part of the Whole

Seeing everything as part of the whole can help us to cultivate empathy and compassion towards others. It can also help us to recognize the interconnectedness of all things and to act in ways that promote harmony and unity, mindfulness and presence.

Cultivating Equal Vision

If we wish to see everything as a part of the whole, mindfulness and meditation are essential. It is also helpful to remain grateful and to practice acts of kindness and service towards others, recognizing that others' well-being is intimately tied to our own.

Conclusion

Amma teaches the interconnectedness of all things and the importance of treating others with love and compassion. By cultivating an understanding of the unity of life, we can live more harmoniously with all beings.

***

90. Mind

"A porter uses his head to carry luggage. Scientists use their heads to unravel the mysteries of the universe." —Amma

Once, a group of PhD students approached Amma during darshan to ask her how to unravel the mysteries of the universe. Amma, as always, had a unique perspective to offer. She emphasized the importance of discernment and spirituality in discovering the ultimate Truth.

PhD Student 1: Amma, I am studying neuroscience, and I want to understand how the brain works. It's so complex and fascinating!

Amma: That's wonderful, dear. The brain is indeed a marvel of creation. But remember, it's not just about using your head to unravel the mysteries of the universe. We also need to use our hearts and our intuition. When we have discernment, we can see beyond the surface level of things and perceive the deeper truths at play.

PhD Student 2: Amma, I want to understand the fundamental laws of nature through my study of Physics to understand how everything is connected.

Amma: You're right, my son. Everything in creation is interconnected and interdependent. It's like the porter who carries luggage on his head - everything is balanced and in harmony. But when we try to understand the universe only through our intellect, we may miss the bigger picture. That's where spirituality comes in - it helps us to see the ultimate Truth that underlies all of creation.

PhD Student 3: Amma, I am studying mathematics, and I want to understand the beauty of numbers and patterns. It's like a language that speaks through the universe.

Amma: It's true. Mathematics is a universal language that can help us understand the order and symmetry in creation. But don't forget, my son, it's not just about the mind and the intellect. We need to cultivate a deeper awareness and consciousness through spiritual practices like meditation and selfless service. Only then can we truly appreciate the beauty of creation and our place in it.

Commentary
The Role of the Porter

Amma begins by comparing the work of a porter to that of a scientist. A porter uses his head to carry luggage. In this example, the porter represents all those who dutifully engage in physical labor to earn a living.

The Work of the Scientist: In contrast, scientists use their heads to unravel the mysteries of the universe. This type of work requires a deep understanding of complex concepts and theories.

Using the Intellect for Positive Outcomes

Amma says that the head can be used to benefit society, whether it is to carry luggage or to unravel the mysteries of the universe. She encourages us all to use our intellects to achieve positive outcomes in our lives, whether it is to render practical service or to pursue knowledge and understanding.

Conclusion

Amma encourages all of us to use our intellects to achieve positive outcomes. At the same time, Amma reminds us of the importance of integrating our heart and intuition as we seek to unravel the mysteries of the universe.

***

91. Relaxation

"Once you learn the art of relaxation, everything happens spontaneously and effortlessly." – Amma

Amma's teachings are not limited to spiritual discourse, but also provide practical guidance for daily life. In one such instance, a brahmachari was meditating near Amma during darshan. She noticed that he looked tense. Later, Amma took the initiative to call him to the beach to share the art of relaxation with him. Amma's compassion extends to every aspect of her devotees' lives.

Amma: Why do you look so tense, my child?

Brahmachari: Amma, I am trying to meditate, but my mind is not calm. I can't relax.

Amma: Relaxation is an art, my child. Once you learn it, everything happens spontaneously and effortlessly. Let me show you how.

Amma walked to the beach with the brahmachari, and they sat down.

Amma: Close your eyes, take a deep breath, and exhale slowly. Now slowly open your eyes and focus on the waves of the ocean. Watch them come and go. Don't think about anything else. Just be present in the moment.

The brahmachari did as Amma said, and slowly began to relax.

Amma: Good. Now, bring that same feeling of relaxation into your daily life. When you feel tense or stressed, take a moment to breathe deeply and focus on the present moment. Remember, relaxation is the key to a peaceful and happy life.

Brahmachari: Thank you, Amma. I will take time to relax every day just like you taught me.

Amma: Good! Remember, my child, I am always here to guide you.

Commentary
The Art of Relaxation

Relaxation is an art that needs to be learned and practiced. It involves letting go of stress and tension in the body and mind. It is a state of being free from worries and anxiety. Amma teaches that relaxation can be achieved through practices such as meditation, yoga, and breathing exercises.

Effortless and Spontaneous Living

Once a person learns the art of relaxation, living becomes more effortless and spontaneous. Relaxation helps us to reduce the burden of worries and anxieties, which in turn leads to a more peaceful and fulfilling life. When the mind is at ease, decision-making becomes easier and our actions become more aligned with our true self.

Benefits of Relaxation

The benefits of relaxation are numerous. It helps to reduce stress and anxiety, which has a positive impact on physical health, mental well-being, and overall quality of life. Relaxation also helps to improve focus, concentration, and productivity.

Incorporating Relaxation into Daily Life

Amma suggests incorporating relaxation techniques into daily life. Some of these include taking short breaks during the day, practicing meditation and yoga, and engaging in hobbies and activities that bring joy and peace.

Conclusion

In this touching interaction with the brahmachari, Amma highlights the importance of relaxation and the positive impact it can have on our lives. By practicing the art of relaxation, we can experience greater levels of peace, fulfillment, and well-being.

92. Selflessness

"Learn to place others before yourself. Consider everyone else first because they are each a doorway to your own Self." —Amma

Once during a lunch stop during a South Indian Tour, Amma's compassion was on full display. She noticed a mother and small child in need of help. She directed one of her brahmachari disciples to assist the mother.

So, the brahmachari went to help, giving them food and asking what other assistance they needed. He took the mother's address, so he could follow up on her welfare after the tour was over. After the mother left, the brahmachari spoke with Amma about the importance of placing others first.

Brahmachari: Amma, I was happy to help the mother with the baby, but I was initially hesitant. I didn't want to disturb you while you were talking with someone else.

Amma: No, no, it's okay. This is what seva is all about. We should always be ready to help others in need. By doing so, we can learn to place others before ourselves.

Brahmachari: Yes, Amma. But sometimes I feel overwhelmed with the amount of seva that needs to be done.

Amma: It's important to remember that every person is a doorway to your own Self. By serving others, we are actually serving ourselves. Learn to do seva without any expectations. When we can do seva with a selfless attitude, everything happens spontaneously and effortlessly.

Brahmachari: Thank you, Amma. I will try my very best to put this into practice.

Amma: Good, my son. Keep up the good work.

Commentary
Placing Others Before Ourselves

Amma constantly emphasizes the value of selflessness. When we perform acts of selfless service, we are cultivating empathy, compassion, and kindness towards others. This allows us to connect with others on a deeper level, and also helps to dissolve the ego, which can be a barrier to spiritual growth.

Seeing Others as a Doorway to the Self

Each person we encounter is a doorway into our own self. When we see others as a part of ourselves, we can learn valuable lessons and gain a greater sense of connectedness and unity with the world around us and a deeper understanding of our own nature.

The Benefits of Considering Others

By considering others first, we develop humility, empathy, and compassion. We learn to see beyond our own narrow perspectives and to understand the perspectives of others. This, in turn, helps us to dissolve the boundaries between us and leads to a greater sense of unity and connectedness.

Conclusion

Amma stresses the importance of placing others before ourselves and of considering everyone as a mirror reflecting us back to ourselves. By doing so, we can cultivate greater empathy, compassion, and selflessness, which can help us to dissolve the ego and connect with others.

***

93. Awareness

"Do your actions with great care and attention and without being consumed by anxiety about the results." – Amma

One night during a tour, as everyone was busily preparing for the program, Amma decided to walk around the pandal site where the program was to be held. As she walked, the organizers approached her to seek her blessing.

Organizers: Amma, we are so busy with preparations for the program. There is so much work to do, and we are feeling anxious about getting everything done on time.

Amma: My children, please do your actions with great care and attention. You must take care to avoid any disasters, but do not worry too much about the results. Do what you can, and leave the rest to God.

Organizers: But Amma, we want everything to be perfect. What if something goes wrong?

Amma: My children, perfection is not in our hands. We can only do our best. Trust in God and have faith that everything will work out as it should.

Commentary
Focus on the Process, Not Just on the Outcome

Amma encourages us to put our full effort into whatever we are doing, focusing on the process of the action, rather than on the end result. By doing so, we can be fully present in the moment and enjoy the task at hand without worrying about the outcome.

Cultivate Detachment from Results

One of Amma's key teachings is about staying detached from the results of our actions. By letting go of our attachment to outcomes, we can free ourselves from anxiety and worry and focus on doing our best in the present moment. This also allows us to accept the outcome, without being attached to a particular result.

Take Responsibility for Your Actions

Amma reminds us that we are responsible for our actions, and that our actions have consequences. By being mindful of our actions and taking responsibility for them, we can create positive change in ourselves and the world.

Embrace Impermanence and Uncertainty

Amma teaches us to embrace the impermanence and uncertainty of life. By accepting that things are constantly changing and not in our control, we can learn to let go of our anxiety and find peace in the present moment.

Conclusion

Amma's consistent encouragement to do actions with care, attention and peaceful detachment, offers a powerful framework for finding inner peace and fulfillment. By focusing on the process, taking responsibility for our actions, and embracing impermanence and uncertainty, we will know greater fulfillment in our work.

***

94. Compassion

"God dwells in the hearts of the compassionate." –Amma

Once as Amma was singing and meditating at the beach, some brahmacharis came near her to ask about God and realization.

Brahmachari 1: Amma, can you tell us how to realize God?

Amma: Realizing God is not like achieving an ordinary goal in life. It is not something that can be attained through a few techniques or practices. It requires a pure heart, selfless service, and compassion.

Brahmachari 2: But Amma, how do we cultivate these qualities?

Amma: By serving others with love and compassion. When we serve others, we see the same divinity that exists within us in every being. It is through this understanding that we realize our true nature.

Brahmachari 3: But Amma, how can we be sure that God exists?

Amma: God is just like the wind. Although we cannot see the wind, we can feel it. God is the same. The presence of God can be felt through the love and compassion that we express towards others.

Brahmachari 4: Amma, what is the purpose of life?

Amma: The purpose of life is to realize our true nature and merge with God. To do this, we must serve others and cultivate compassion.

Brahmachari 1: Thank you for your guidance, Amma.

Amma: My dear children, always remember that God dwells in the hearts of the compassionate. Serve others with love and compassion, and you will experience the presence of God in every moment of your life.

Commentary

Amma's teachings reflect the wisdom of the ancient Indian scriptures and focus on developing qualities such as selflessness, compassion, and gratitude. In fact, one of Amma's core messages is the importance of developing a compassionate heart, which is reflected in her reminder that "God dwells in the hearts of the compassionate."

The Importance of Compassion

Compassion is the foundation of all spiritual practices and the key to living a life of meaning and purpose. By cultivating compassion, we open our hearts to others, and come to understand the world and ourselves in a profound way.

Developing a Compassionate Heart

Amma's teachings emphasize the importance of developing a compassionate heart. This involves learning to see others as extensions of ourselves and recognizing their suffering as our own. When we develop a compassionate heart, we become less judgmental and more accepting of others, which fosters a sense of peace and harmony.

The Benefits of Compassion

Compassion has many benefits, both for ourselves and for others. When we cultivate compassion, we become more empathetic and understanding, and this helps us to connect more deeply with others. Compassion also helps us to overcome negative emotions such as anger, jealousy, and greed.

Living a Life of Service

One of the key ways to develop a compassionate heart is through service to others. Amma's teachings emphasize the importance of living a life of service and helping those who are less fortunate. By serving others, we develop a deeper sense of empathy and compassion, and this helps us to connect more deeply with others.

Embodying Amma's Teachings

To truly embody the message of Amma's teachings, we must make compassion the cornerstone of our lives by practicing kindness, empathy, and understanding in all of our interactions with others and working to alleviate suffering wherever we can.

Conclusion

Amma's message of compassion is a powerful reminder of the importance of kindness, empathy, and understanding in our lives. By developing a compassionate heart and living a life of service, we can bring more peace and harmony to the world.

***

95. Hope
"Always remember that when dusk arrives, it already has dawn in its womb." —Amma

Once as Amma was spending time with the ashram residents watching the sunset at the beach, the residents asked her questions about the meaning of life and death, and the correct way to perceive them. With infinite compassion and love, Amma gave insightful answers and helped them find solace.

Amma: (*smiling*) I am happy to see you all here. The sunset is so beautiful, isn't it?

Resident 1: (*looking at the sunset*) Amma, what is life?

Amma: Life is a precious gift given to us by the Divine. We should use this gift to help others and make the world a better place. Life is an opportunity to serve and realize the Self.

Resident 2: (*looking a bit worried*) Amma, what about death? What happens after we die?

Amma: Death is a natural part of life. Just as the sun sets in the evening, our bodies too will one day rest in peace. But our souls are eternal, and they will continue on their journey towards the ultimate Truth. We should not fear death but prepare ourselves for it by living a life of love and service.

Resident 3: (*curiously*) Amma, how can we see life and death in the right way?

Amma: (*smiling*) To see life and death in the right way, we need to have faith, hope, and understanding. We should have faith in the Divine, hope for a better future, and understanding of the impermanence of this world. We should always remember that when dusk arrives, it already has dawn in its womb. Life and death are just different aspects of the same journey towards the ultimate Truth.

Commentary

In this dialogue, Amma reminds us to remain hopeful and positive even in times of darkness. She suggests that even in such times, there is always hope for a brighter future. Just as dusk gives way to dawn, even the darkest moments can be followed by brighter times.

Finding Hope in Difficult Times: Amma encourages us to look for hope even when things seem bleak. Whether we are facing personal challenges or global crises, there is always the possibility of positive change. By maintaining a hopeful attitude, we can stay motivated and work towards a better future.

The Power of Positive Thinking

Amma's words highlight the importance of positive thinking. By focusing on hope and remaining positive, we can create a more optimistic outlook. This can lead to greater resilience in the face of challenges and a more fulfilling life overall.

Hope and a Positive Outlook

Throughout her teachings, Amma emphasizes the importance of cultivating a positive outlook on life. She encourages her followers to practice gratitude, to seek out the good in others, to and maintain a sense of hope even in difficult times.

Conclusion

Amma reminds us that even in the darkest of times, there is always the possibility of hope and better things to come. By remaining hopeful, we invite a better future.

***

96. Nature

"Mother Earth is always serving us. The sun, the moon and the stars all serve us. What can we do in return for their selfless service?" – Amma

As a spiritual leader and environmentalist, Amma has always emphasized the importance of living in harmony with nature. She constantly reminds us of our duty to protect the environment and to take only what is necessary from nature. During one of her beach meditations, Amma was approached by some residents who sought her guidance on how to maintain the ecosystem and use natural resources judiciously. Amma's response was insightful and filled with wisdom.

Amma: This is a very important question. Mother Earth and all of nature are constantly serving us selflessly. We are receiving so much from Her, but what can we do in return?

Resident 1: How can we reduce our impact on the environment and live in harmony with nature?

Amma: One way is to be mindful of our consumption. We should take only what we need and not waste resources. We should also be mindful of the products we use and their impact on the environment. For example, we can use natural and biodegradable products instead of synthetic ones.

Resident 2: What else can we do to protect the environment?

Amma: We can also participate in environmental activities and initiatives in our local community. Planting trees, cleaning up beaches and rivers, and supporting conservation efforts are just a few ways we can give back to nature. And most importantly, we should cultivate a sense of gratitude and respect towards nature.

Resident 3: How can we teach others to be more mindful of the environment?

Amma: The best way to teach others is by example. If we live our lives in a mindful and respectful way towards nature, others will see the positive impact and be inspired to follow. We should also share our knowledge and experiences with others and encourage them to do the same. Remember, every action we take towards protecting the environment is a step towards a healthier world.

Commentary
Ways to Give Back to Mother Earth
Amma suggests various ways in which we can give back to the Earth, such as reducing our carbon footprint, conserving resources, planting trees, and supporting organizations that protect the environment.

The Benefits of Serving the Earth
Amma emphasizes that by serving the Earth and its inhabitants, we not only show our gratitude but also benefit from the positive impact. If we are grateful, Mother Nature will take care of our welfare and the well-being of future generations.

Conclusion
Our connection to the Earth is deep and profound, and it is our responsibility to care for Mother Nature with love and respect. By recognizing the selfless service of the Earth and all its inhabitants, we can cultivate a greater sense of gratitude and learn to give back. Through our actions, we can create a better future for all.

***

97. Love

"Love and beauty are within you. Try to express them through your actions, and you will definitely touch the very source of bliss." – Amma

During a visit to Reunion Island, a group of devotees asked Amma to share her thoughts on beauty, love, and bliss. They were eager to learn whether these concepts were interrelated or separate.

Devotee 1: Amma, we are surrounded by so much beauty here on this island. Is beauty separate from love and bliss, or are they all connected?

Amma: My child, love and beauty are not separate from each other. They both originate from the same source of consciousness. When you appreciate the beauty around you, it awakens a feeling of love in your heart. When love awakens, it leads you to experience the ultimate state of bliss. So, beauty, love, and bliss are all interconnected.

Devotee 2: But Amma, how can we express this love and beauty through our actions?

Amma: My dear child, every action we take can be an expression of love and beauty. When you perform your actions with mindfulness and compassion, your actions become beautiful. When your actions are beautiful, they can inspire others to experience love and beauty in their lives.

Devotee 3: Amma, how can we touch the very source of bliss that you speak of?

Amma: The source of bliss is within each one of us. It is the true nature of the Self. By turning inward through meditation and self-inquiry, we can connect with the source of bliss within ourselves. When we touch that source of bliss, we are able to experience love, beauty, and joy in every moment of our lives.

Commentary
Amma encourages us to find love and beauty within ourselves and to express it in all of our actions.

Love and Beauty Are Inherent Within Us
Amma teaches that love and beauty are not external qualities that one needs to search for outside. Instead, they are innate qualities that are already present within us. By recognizing and nurturing these qualities, we can experience true happiness and fulfillment.

Expressing Love and Beauty Through Actions: Amma invites us to express love and beauty through our actions. Even small acts of kindness, compassion, and selfless service can have a profound impact on others and the world around us. By making a conscious effort to express these qualities in our daily lives, we can make a positive difference in the world and create a ripple effect of goodness.

Attaining True Happiness and Bliss
Amma suggests that by expressing love and beauty through our actions, we can experience true happiness and bliss. Material possessions or external achievements may provide temporary happiness, but lasting fulfillment comes from within. By connecting with our innate qualities of love and beauty, we can experience a deep sense of contentment and inner peace.

Self-Improvement and Inner Transformation
Amma often emphasize the importance of self-improvement and inner transformation. By cultivating positive qualities within ourselves, such as love, compassion, and selflessness, we can become better individuals and contribute positively to the world. Through regular spiritual practice and self-reflection, we can strive towards our highest potential.

Conclusion

Amma's call to find love and beauty within ourselves and to express these qualities through actions is a powerful reminder of our innate goodness. By cultivating love and beauty within ourselves and making a conscious effort to express them in our daily lives, we can create a positive impact and come to know true happiness.

***

98. Enlightenment

"Enlightenment means the ability to recognize oneself in all living creatures." —Amma

People from all walks of life seek Amma's guidance and wisdom, hoping to deepen their understanding of themselves and the world around them. In this encounter, a devotee flips the tables and asks Amma how she sees herself and the world.

Devotee: Amma, who are you and how do you perceive the world?

Amma: Who are you? Know yourself, then you will know Amma.

Devotee: But Amma, I don't understand.

Amma: Enlightenment means the ability to recognize oneself in all living creatures. You are not just your body or mind. You are the Atman, the eternal Self. When you realize this, you will see that the same divinity that exists within you, exists within everyone and everything.

Devotee: Hmmm...I see, Amma. But how can I recognize this divinity within myself and others?

Amma: Through selfless service, love, and compassion. When you serve others, you are serving the divinity that exists within them. And when you see this divinity within others, you will automatically see it within yourself as well. This is the path to enlightenment.

Devotee: Thank you, Amma. I will try to practice this in my life.

Amma: My child, always remember that the key to enlightenment lies within you. Keep walking the path of love and selfless service, and you will surely reach the ultimate goal.

Commentary

In this conversation, Amma defines enlightenment as recognizing one's unity with all living creatures.

Self-Realization

Amma describes enlightenment as the ability to recognize our true selves. The journey towards self-realization is the process of becoming more and more aware of our true nature beyond the ego.

Connection with All Living Creatures

Amma's words suggest that enlightenment involves recognizing ourselves in all living creatures and developing a deep connection with the world around us. To reach this goal, we must deeply imbibe the truth that we are not separate from the universe, but rather a part of it.

Compassion and Empathy

Recognizing oneself in others naturally brings a sense of compassion and empathy towards all living creatures. As we begin to understand the interconnectedness of all things, our hearts become more and more expansive.

Recognizing Ourselves in Others

When we perceive ourselves in all living creatures, we break down barriers of separation and isolation. We begin to understand that we are all one, and that the suffering of one is the suffering of all.

Conclusion

Amma's words about the nature of enlightenment, challenge us to see ourselves in all living creatures and to develop a deep sense of interconnectedness, compassion, and empathy. It is a journey that eventually leads us to a profound understanding of the world around us.

***

99. Mind

"When the waves of the mind subside, you will see that everything you seek is already within you." – Amma

During one of her visits to the beach, Amma's stillness inspired the residents to seek guidance on realizing the Self. The ensuing dialogue between Amma and the residents centered on the need for meditation and self-reflection.

Resident 1: Amma, how can we realize our true Self?

Amma: You can start by keeping your mind in a peaceful and balanced condition. Then listen to teachings about the Self from a teacher or the scriptures and reflect upon them. Meditate on that knowledge until you have a deep conviction of its truth.

Resident 2: But Amma, how do we keep our mind in a peaceful state when there are so many distractions and thoughts?

Amma: By constant practice, we can train our mind to become still and focused. One effective way is through regular meditation. The more we practice, the easier it becomes to quiet the mind and experience inner peace.

Resident 3: Amma, what is the role of surrender in realizing the Self?

Amma: Surrender is a vital aspect of spiritual practice. When we surrender our ego and desires to the divine, we open ourselves up to receiving grace and guidance from this higher power. It helps us to let go of our attachments and find peace in the present moment.

Resident 4: Amma, can you give us an example of how to apply these teachings in daily life?

Amma: Yes, you can try to practice japa and Self-awareness throughout your day. Observe your thoughts and actions, and try to align them with your highest values. You can also engage in seva (selfless service) as a way to purify your mind and cultivate compassion towards others. Remember, everything you seek is already within you. You just need to quiet the mind and realize the truth.

As Amma sat serenely on the beach, the sound of the roaring waves created a soothing effect. The residents sat in deep silence, absorbing the peace that radiated from Amma's presence. Gradually, Amma returned to the present moment exuding love and compassion.

One resident finally gathered up the courage to break the silence and ask a question.

Resident 1: Amma, how can we realize the Self?

Amma: Keep the mind in a condition to hear about the Self. Reflect on what you hear and meditate on it until conviction comes.

Resident 2: Amma, what is the Self?

Amma: The Self is the essence of who we are, beyond the body, mind, and emotions. It is the eternal consciousness that exists in all living beings.

Resident 3: But Amma, how can we know the Self?

Amma: Through selfless service, devotion, and surrender to the divine. When the mind becomes still and free from distractions, the Self can be realized. The path to realizing the Self is not easy, but with sincere effort and grace, it is possible. Keep faith, and the divine will reveal itself to you.

Commentary

Amma' words encourage us to still our minds and look within. It is only there we will find everything we seek. As Amma herself says, "When the waves of the mind subside you will see that everything you seek is already within you."

Stilling the Mind

Amma encourages us to still the mind in order to gain clarity and peace. By learning to calm the mind, we can let go of stress, access our inner wisdom and connect with our true selves.

Looking Within
Although Amma says that everything we seek is already within us, we often look outside of ourselves to find happiness, success, and fulfillment. When we finally learn to quiet our minds and connect with our inner selves, we will be able to tap into a source of infinite wisdom, peace, and joy.

Understanding Our True Nature
Stilling the mind and looking within can help us understand our true nature. We are not just our thoughts, emotions, and physical bodies, but something much more profound. By connecting with our true nature, our lives take on a rich sense of meaning and purpose.

How to still the mind
Amma suggests many ways to still the mind, such as meditation, yoga, mindfulness practices, and spending time in nature. Amma encourages each of us to experiment, find the methods that resonate best with us, and make them a part of our daily routine.

Benefits of stilling the mind
Stilling the mind has numerous benefits. It reduces stress and anxiety, increases focus and concentration, improves overall well-being, and enhances spiritual growth. A still mind, brings with it the gifts of peace, clarity, and joy.

Conclusion
Amma's seaside words encourage us to still our minds and look within ourselves to find everything we seek. By learning to calm the mind, joy, peace, inner wisdom, and a sense of connection with our true Self begins to blossom.

***

100. Equanimity
"The ability to retain equanimity of mind in all circumstances is what makes a successful life." —Amma

Amma believes that the key to a successful life lies not in external actions, but in the ability to maintain equanimity of mind in all circumstances. In the following conversation with her ashram residents, Amma emphasizes the importance of having a Guru's presence and guidance in our lives

Amma: Dear ones, we often think that we need to go to the Himalayas or take dips in the Ganga to find spiritual enlightenment. But the truth is, it's not the external pilgrimage that matters, it's the inner journey that counts. And the presence of a Guru and their guidance can help you on that path. The ability to retain equanimity of mind in all circumstances is what makes a successful life.

Resident 1: But Amma, how do we find such a Guru? And how do we know if their guidance is right for us?

Amma: The Guru will find you when you are ready, my child. And you will know if their guidance is right for you because you will feel it in your heart. You will feel a deep resonance with their teaching. Once the bond is established, they will help you to connect with your innermost self.

Resident 2: But Amma, how do we maintain equanimity of mind in all circumstances? Life is so full of challenges and ups and downs.

Amma: It's true, life can be difficult at times, but it's important to remember that everything is impermanent. The good times will pass, but so will the bad times. And if we can cultivate a sense of detachment from our experiences, we can maintain equanimity of mind. We can observe our thoughts and emotions without getting caught up in them. And with the help of a Guru, we can develop this ability further.

Resident 3: Amma, how can we develop this detachment and equanimity of mind? Is it through meditation?

Amma: Until we get conviction that Self is ever free, meditation on the Self is certainly one way to develop this ability, but it's not the only way. It's about cultivating awareness in every moment, about being present with whatever is happening without judgment or attachment. It's about developing a deeper understanding of the nature of reality and our place within it. And with the help of a Guru, we can deepen our understanding and cultivate the ability to maintain equanimity of mind in all circumstances.

Commentary

One of Amma's most important teachings is about maintaining equanimity of mind in all circumstances.

Equanimity of Mind

Equanimity refers to the ability to remain calm and composed in the face of adversity or challenging situations. Amma teaches that developing this quality is essential to leading a successful life.

Importance of Equanimity

Amma stresses the importance of maintaining equanimity in all areas of life, including personal relationships, work, and spiritual practice. She believes that only a balanced and peaceful mind will lead us to success in all of these areas.

Attaining Equanimity

Amma teaches that developing equanimity requires practice, discipline, and a strong connection with the inner Self. She recommends techniques such as meditation, self-reflection, and selfless service to help cultivate this quality.

Benefits of Equanimity

By developing equanimity, one can experience great mental clarity, emotional stability, and spiritual growth. Amma explains that a calm mind reduces stress and anxiety, improves decision-making, and deepens our connection to the Divine.

Conclusion

Amma invites us to develop equanimity of mind in all circumstances, which will bring greater inner peace and balance. By developing this quality, we can overcome the challenges of life with a sense of ease, grace, joy, love, and fulfillment.

***

101. Humility

"If you become a zero, you become a hero." —Amma

Once as Amma was addressing a group of politicians from Madhya Pradesh, they asked her how to lead the country. Amma replied with her famous quote, "If you become a zero, you become a hero." The politicians were intrigued and asked Amma to elaborate on what she meant.

Politician 1: Amma, I'm having trouble understanding what you mean by becoming a zero. Can you explain it to us in more detail?

Amma: Yes, son. By becoming a zero, I mean letting go of your ego and all the attachments that come with it. When you empty yourself of all your personal desires and ambitions, you become a vessel for the divine to work through. This is the key to true success and leadership.

Politician 2: But Amma, we are politicians. We need to have a certain level of ambition and drive in order to succeed in our careers.

Amma: Of course, ambition is important, but it must be tempered by humility and a willingness to serve others. When you put the needs of your people before your own desires, you become a true leader.

Politician 3: Amma, how can we ensure that we stay humble and focused on serving others while we're in power?

Amma: The key is to stay connected to your spiritual practice and your Guru. When you have a strong foundation of spiritual discipline, you'll be able to stay centered and focused on what's truly important, even in the face of power and success.

Politician 4: Amma, I'm worried that if I let go of my ego, I won't be able to stand up to my opponents and fight for what I believe in.

Amma: There's a difference between standing up for what's right and fighting for your own personal gain. When you become a zero, you'll be able to discern the difference and act accordingly. Remember, true power comes from within, not from external sources.

Commentary

In this dynamic conversation, Amma challenges us to be zeros to become heroes. It's her way of saying we should cultivate humility and detachment in our lives.

Cultivating Humility

Amma teaches that humility is essential on the spiritual path. When we become attached to our ego and self-importance, we create suffering for ourselves and others. By becoming a zero, we let go of our ego and become open to the divine presence within us.

Detachment

Amma emphasizes the importance of detachment and non-attachment in spiritual practice. When we become attached to material possessions or relationships, we limit our spiritual growth. By becoming a zero, we let go of our attachment to worldly things and open ourselves up to the infinite potential of the universe.

Embracing the Unknown

Becoming a zero means embracing the unknown and being open to new experiences. When we let go of our preconceptions and judgments, we can approach life with a sense of wonder and curiosity. This opens us up to discover innovative solutions. When we become a zero, we allow ourselves to be guided by the divine presence within us and experience life in a richer way.

Conclusion

Amma's famous quote, "If you become a zero, you become a hero," encourages us to cultivate humility, detachment, and openness in our lives. By letting go of our ego and attachment to worldly things, we learn to connect with the divine presence within us and to experience life in a more meaningful way. Becoming a zero is not about losing ourselves or giving up our individuality, but about opening ourselves up to a greater sense of purpose and potential.

***

102. Self

"You own the entire universe. Throw away your begging bowl and look for the treasure hidden within you." – Amma

Some years ago, as Amma was surrounded by sadhus from the Vivekananda lineage, her mind turned to India. In that moment, she spoke with great love and respect for Mother India and then encouraged the sadhus to abandon their material possessions and to search within for the true treasure, the light of the Self.

Sadhu 1: Amma, we have left our families, possessions, and worldly pleasures to seek the path of truth. But we still feel like something is missing. What is this treasure within that you speak of?

Amma: The treasure within is the awareness of your own true nature, the Self. It is the source of all joy, peace, and love. You already own the entire universe, but you are not aware of it. Once you discover the treasure within, you will realize your true potential.

Sadhu 2: But Amma, we have renounced everything. How can we look for treasure when we have nothing?

Amma: You don't need anything external to find this treasure. In fact, the external world can distract you from finding it. Throw away your begging bowl, let go of all desires and attachments, and turn inward. The treasure is hidden within you, waiting to be discovered.

Sadhu 3: Amma, we are like soldiers on a battlefield, fighting against ignorance and illusion. How can we abandon everything and focus on the Self?

Amma: Your bravery is admirable, but remember that the battle is within. To win this battle, you must first recognize your own true nature. The awareness of the Self will give you the strength and clarity to fight with renewed vigor.

Sadhu 4: Amma, we are grateful for your guidance. But how do we know if we are on the right path?

Amma: The path of the Self is a path of love, compassion, and service. When you are on the right path, you will feel an inner joy and peace that cannot be described. Keep walking with faith and devotion, and the treasure within will reveal itself to you.

The sadhus bowed their heads in great respect.

Commentary

Amma urges us to look within to discover the greatest of hidden treasures.

The Universe is Within You

Amma reminds us that every individual is connected to the universe and that we must recognize this to tap into our infinite potential.

Throw Away Your Begging Bowl

Amma encourages people to let go of their attachment to external possessions and to instead focus on the treasure within.

Look for the Treasure Within

Amma stresses the importance of self-discovery and introspection to find the true essence within.

Conclusion

Amma's message encourages people to tap into their inner strength and to recognize their unlimited potential. By letting go of attachments to external possessions and focusing on the treasure within, individuals can at last find fulfillment.

***

103. Attitude
"We cannot change situations in life, but we can change our attitude towards them." — Amma

One day a brahmachari came to Amma with a problem. He was building houses for the poor, as part of Amma's Amrita Kuteeram project, but he was facing challenges. The local people were not coming to help in the construction project. The brahmachari was feeling discouraged and upset.

Brahmachari: Amma, nobody is changing. When I went to build houses for the poor, the local people did not help at all. They just watched; this really upset me!

Amma: My dear child, we cannot change others, but we can change our attitude towards them. Instead of focusing on what others are not doing, let us focus on what we can do to help those in need.

Brahmachari: But Amma, I feel like I'm alone in this project. I need the support of others to make a real difference.

Amma: Remember, my child, that change starts with one person. If you continue to work with dedication and love, others will be inspired to join you. Even if no one else helps you, continue to work with a positive attitude and a spirit of service. Your efforts will not go in vain.

Brahmachari: Thank you, Amma. I will keep trying.

Amma: Always remember, my child, that the work we do for others is not just about building houses or helping those in need. It is also about transforming ourselves and cultivating a spirit of compassion and selflessness. May your efforts be blessed with success, and may you always serve with a heart full of love.

Commentary
Challenging Situations

Life is full of ups and downs. We all face challenging situations from time. Amma reminds us that although we cannot change the situations themselves, we can change our attitude towards them. By doing so, we can transform difficult situations into opportunities for growth and self-discovery.

The Power of Attitude

Our attitude plays a crucial role in how we experience life. If we approach difficult situations with a negative attitude, we are likely to feel overwhelmed and defeated. However, if we cultivate a positive attitude, we empower ourselves to find solutions to even the most challenging problems.

Strategies for Changing Our Attitude

Amma suggests several strategies for changing our attitude towards challenging situations, including developing a sense of detachment, practicing mindfulness and meditation, focusing on gratitude, and embracing the present moment.

Benefits of Changing Our Attitude

When we change our attitude towards challenging situations, we experience many benefits. We feel more in control of our lives, more confident in our ability to handle difficulties, and more compassionate towards ourselves and others. We also experience greater peace of mind and an increased sense of inner joy and contentment.

Living in Harmony with Life's Ups and Downs

Ultimately, the key to living a fulfilling life is to embrace all of life's experiences, both positive and negative. By changing our attitude towards challenging situations, we can learn to live in harmony with life's ups and downs and to find meaning and purpose in every moment.

Conclusion

Amma teaches that we cannot change the situations in life, but we can change our attitude towards them. This important reminder empowers us to transform even the most challenging situations into opportunities for growth and self-discovery. By cultivating a positive attitude and embracing life's ups and downs, we put ourselves back in touch with the peace and joy that are our true nature.

***

104. Attitude

"A situation becomes a problem only when you interpret it in the wrong way." – Amma

Misunderstandings can often lead to strained relationships and conflicts, even between people who share a common spiritual path. In the following dialogue, a brahmachari approaches Amma with a predicament. He had accused a fellow brahmachari of misplacing his things, which led to a rift between them.

Amma: (*gently*) Why did you assume your brahmachari brother misplaced your things?

Brahmachari: Amma, I saw that my things had been moved from where I left them. And since the other brahmachari often uses those things, I assumed he had misplaced them.

Amma: (*smiling*) But you see, assuming and jumping to conclusions without verifying the facts can lead to misunderstandings and unnecessary conflicts. It's important to approach situations with an open mind and not let our assumptions cloud our judgment.

Brahmachari: I realize my mistake now, Amma. I should have checked with him first instead of assuming the worst.

Amma; (*nodding in agreement*) Indeed, the situation only became a problem because you interpreted it in the wrong way. Let this be a lesson for all of us to always verify the facts before jumping to conclusions.

Commentary

Amma reminds us that our attitude towards situations can make all the difference.

The Power of Interpretation

Amma suggests that it is not situations in themselves that are the problem, but rather our interpretation of them. By changing our perspective, we can transform challenging situations into opportunities for growth.

The Importance of Attitude

Our attitude towards any given situation has a significant impact on how we experience it. A positive attitude can help us to find solutions and move forward, while a negative attitude invariably create more problems.

The Role of Mindfulness

Mindfulness helps us to become more aware of our thoughts and interpretations of events. By practicing mindfulness, we can learn to observe our reactions and choose more positive interpretations of the situations we encounter.

Conclusion

Amma reminds us that we have the power to shape our experiences by changing our attitudes and interpretations. By focusing on the positive and practicing mindfulness, we can transform challenging situations into learning opportunities.

***

105. Happiness

"Happiness is a decision—a firm decision that 'Whatever comes in life, I will be happy.'" –Amma

Amma was visiting a beach in North India, where a group of devotees had gathered to hear her speak. Like crashing waves, the devotees vied for Amma's attention. But Amma somehow managed to reach out and bless each wave with her love. The devotees eagerly listened as Amma shared her wisdom on the topic of happiness.

Devotee 1: Amma, how can we find happiness in this world?

Amma: Happiness is not something you find, my child. It is a decision that you make. A firm decision that no matter what comes your way, you will choose to be happy.

Devotee 2: But Amma, how can we be happy when there is so much suffering in the world?

Amma: By learning to see the divine in every person and in every situation. When we see the divine in everything, we can find peace and joy even in difficult times.

Devotee 3: Amma, what can we do to find inner peace?

Amma: Meditation and prayer are the keys to finding inner peace. By stilling the mind and turning our attention inward, we can connect with the divine and find the peace that lies within us.

Devotee 4: Amma, sometimes it feels like life is too difficult to handle. What can we do to overcome these challenges?

Amma: When you face challenges, you must remember your true source, the divine light within you. By connecting with that source, you will find the strength and peace to overcome any difficulty and to choose happiness.

As the conversation continued and the waves continued to roll up onto the shore, each one seemed to be reaching out to touch Amma, as if seeking her blessings.

Commentary

Happiness is a decision that we can make, no matter what our life circumstances. Amma urges us to take control of our emotions and mindset and to choose happiness

Choosing Happiness:

Amma suggests that happiness is not contingent on external factors, such as wealth or success. Rather, it is a decision that one makes despite their life circumstances. By choosing to be happy, individuals can transcend their hardships and find joy in even the most challenging situations.

Cultivating a Positive Mindset

Cultivating a positive mindset is essential to achieving happiness. To develop such a mindset, Amma suggests we live in the present moment, practice gratitude, and reframe our negative thoughts. By training the mind to see the good in every situation, we can shift our perspective and find happiness in even the most mundane tasks.

Overcoming Adversity

Amma teaches that inner strength is essential to achieving happiness. By developing resilience, we can overcome adversity and find joy in the face of challenges. To be successful in this, we must cultivate a sense of purpose and a strong support system.

The Pursuit of Happiness

Amma says happiness is essential to living a fulfilling life. This involves setting goals, pursuing passions, and prioritizing relationships. By living a life aligned with our values, we can experience a sense of fulfillment and lasting happiness.

Conclusion

Amma often reminds us that "happiness is a decision." By focusing on the present moment, cultivating a positive mindset, and developing inner strength, we can find joy and fulfillment despite our life circumstances.

***

106. Pain
"Even painful experiences, when understood deeply, can have a positive effect on our life." —Amma

During darshan in Trivandrum, a devotee approached Amma with a heavy heart. He had been dealing with a great tragedy in his life and was struggling to come to terms with the pain and loss he was feeling. Amma listened patiently as the devotee shared his story.

Devotee: Amma, I am going through a very difficult time. My family has suffered a great tragedy, and I am struggling to cope.

Amma: My child, tell me what has happened.

The devotee opened his heart and shared his pain with Amma, recounting the details of the tragedy that had befallen his family. As Amma listened with compassion, her eyes filled with tears.

Amma: I am so sorry for your pain, my child. But know that even painful experiences, when deeply understood, can have a positive effect on our lives. This too shall pass, and you will emerge stronger from this experience.

The devotee felt a sense of comfort in Amma's words and left the darshan feeling a bit lighter and a bit more at peace. He continued to reflect on Amma's words long after she left Trivandrum and slowly began to see the situation in a new light, recognizing the potential for growth and transformation that lay buried in the experience. Though the pain did not disappear overnight, the devotee felt a newfound sense of hope and resilience, knowing that he had Amma's love and support to carry him through.

Commentary
Understanding Painful Experiences

Amma teaches that pain and suffering are a natural part of life, and we cannot avoid them completely. Painful experiences can take many forms-- physical, emotional, and spiritual. They may arise from loss, disappointment, rejection, or other difficult circumstances.

Learning from Painful Experiences

Amma sees painful experiences as valuable opportunities to learn and grow. When we face challenges, we can ask ourselves what lessons there are to learn from the situation. Perhaps difficult situations are there to teach us empathy, resilience, or wisdom.

Overcoming Painful Experiences

While painful experiences can be valuable, they can also have negative effects on our lives. We may become stuck in negative patterns of thought or behavior, or we may develop a fear of future pain. Amma teaches that by practicing mindfulness, meditation, and self-reflection, we can often overcome these negative effects and move forward with our lives.

Finding the Positive in Painful Experiences

Amma teaches that painful experiences can have positive effects on our lives. They can help us to appreciate the good things in life, deepen our relationships, and spur us to cultivate gratitude. By shifting our perspective and finding the positive aspects of painful experiences, we can transform them into opportunities for growth and healing.

Applying Amma's Teachings

By applying Amma teachings in our lives, we can start by becoming more mindful of our reactions to painful experiences. We can practice self-compassion and self-care, seek support from loved ones, and use our experiences to deepen our understanding of ourselves and others. By living Amma's teachings, we can transform our pain into wisdom and compassion.

Conclusion

Amma provides an invaluable perspective on how to cope with the challenges of life. By understanding the nature of pain, learning from our experiences, and finding the positive in difficult situations, we can grow and thrive in the face of life's challenges.

***

107. Serving

"Children, never waste an opportunity to serve. The entire world looks up to those who have the heart to do selfless service." –Amma

The ashram founded by Amma in Kerala, India, is a hub of humanitarian activities dedicated to the spiritual and social upliftment of all. Amma has always encouraged her followers to engage in selfless service, which is a crucial aspect of spiritual practice. In the following conversation, Amma counsels a brahmachari and ashram resident who are wasting time, doing no selfless service or sadhana whatsoever. Concerned for their well-being, Amma shares words of guidance and encouragement with them.

Amma: My dear children, I have noticed that you are spending much of your time in idleness. Remember, every moment is a precious opportunity to serve others and to deepen your spiritual practice.

Brahmachari: But Amma, we don't know how to serve. We don't have any skills.

Amma: Nonsense! You have the most important skill of all – a kind and compassionate heart. Use that to reach out to those around you and offer them whatever help you can. Even a simple act of kindness can make a huge difference in someone's life.

Resident: But what if we make mistakes? What if we do something wrong?

Amma: Mistakes are part of the learning process, my child. Don't be afraid to make them. Just be sincere in your efforts, and always strive to do your best. Remember, the entire world looks up to those who have the heart to do selfless service. Don't waste this precious opportunity that has been given to you.

With Amma's guidance, the Brahmachari and resident began to engage more fully in the life of the ashram, serving others and deepening their own spiritual practice. They found that by focusing on selfless service, they were able to cultivate a sense of purpose and fulfillment that they had never experienced before.

Commentary
The importance of selfless service cannot be overstated. Amma believes that serving others is the key to finding happiness and purpose in life. In this touching interaction, Amma encourages her children to develop a habit of serving others and to never waste any opportunity to do so.

Selfless Service
Amma says that selfless service is the foundation of spirituality and is crucial for personal growth and development. Serving others helps us to step out of our own self-interests and to connect with the needs of others. It helps us to cultivate the compassion, empathy, and selflessness that are essential for a meaningful living.

The Impact of Serving Others
When we serve others, not only do we help them, but we ourselves also experience a sense of fulfillment and satisfaction. When we serve others, we expand our consciousness and become aware of our interconnectedness with the world. Through selfless service, we can make a positive impact on society and bring about meaningful change.

The Role of Children in Serving Society
Amma believes that children have a significant role to play in serving society. By developing this habit at a young age, young ones can become responsible and empathetic individuals who contribute positively to society. Children who learn the value of selfless service will grow up to be compassionate, selfless leaders who will work for the betterment of society.

Cultivating the Habit of Selfless Service

Amma encourages everyone to cultivate the habit of selfless service in their daily lives. She suggests that serving others should become a way of life rather than an occasional hobby. By making selfless service a habit, we will know the joy of giving and find a deeper sense of purpose.

Seizing Opportunities to Serve

Amma reminds us that opportunities for selfless service are all around us. We just need to be vigilant and seize opportunities to serve whenever possible. She encourages us to be aware and to find opportunities to serve in our daily lives, whether it's helping a neighbor, volunteering at a local charity, or simply listening to someone who needs a compassionate ear.

Conclusion

Amma encourages all of us to make selfless service a way of life and encourages children to develop the habit of serving others early on. She suggests that serving others helps us to grow and develop and creates a positive impact on society. By seizing opportunities to serve, we invite happiness, purpose, and fulfillment into our lives.

***

108. Love
"We are all beads strung together on the same thread of love." —Amma

One day, a group of pandits from North India came to seek Amma's guidance on spiritual matters. They had heard about Amma's profound wisdom and were eager to receive her blessings.

Pandit 1: Amma, how can we cultivate love in our hearts for others?

Amma: Love is the very essence of our being. It is the thread that binds all of us together. Just like beads on a string, we are all connected through the thread of love. To cultivate love towards others, we must first realize our oneness with them. When we see everyone as an extension of ourselves, love automatically flows from our hearts.

Pandit 2: Amma, what is the ultimate goal of spirituality?

Amma: The ultimate goal of spirituality is to realize our true nature, which is the same as the ultimate reality of the universe. The Upanishads say, 'Brahman is everything, and everything is Brahman.' We must realize that we are not separate from the divine, but rather, we are a part of it. When we realize this, we experience infinite joy, peace, and love.

The Pandits continued peppering Amma questions. She patiently answered each one.

Pandit 3: Amma, we want to know more about the nature of the Self.

Amma: Ah, the Self... The Upanishads teach us that the Self is everything. It is the one divine reality that underlies all of creation.

Pandit: But how can we realize this Self?

Amma: By understanding that everything is connected. Just as each bead on a mala is connected by the thread that runs through it, we are all connected by the thread of love that runs through us.

Pandit: Amma, how can we cultivate this love?

Amma: By serving others selflessly. When we serve others, we forget our own ego and merge with the divine. We become one with the love that runs through all of creation.

Pandit: Amma, can you tell us more about this oneness?

Amma: In the *Bhagavad Gita,* Lord Krishna says that He is the thread that runs through all beings. We are all His creations, and He is the one divine reality that unites us all.

Pandit: Amma, this is all so profound. How can we apply this in our daily lives?

Amma: By seeing the divine in all beings and treating them with love and compassion. When we do this, we will find that our own lives are transformed, and we will experience a deep and abiding peace.

Commentary

Over the last forty years, Amma has imparted an ocean of wisdom through her speeches and writings. Among her most memorable quotes of all is, "We are all beads strung together on the same thread of love." It is Amma's way of pointing to our interconnectedness and the importance of cultivating love and compassion towards all.

The Concept of Interconnectedness

Amma teaches that all beings are interconnected, which means that what affects one person, also affects others. For this reason, Amma encourages us to see ourselves as part of a larger whole and to recognize that the well-being of one person is interconnected with the well-being of others.

The Power of Love and Compassion

Amma emphasizes the importance of love and compassion towards others. Love and compassion are the way to connect with others on a deeper level. These qualities also inspire us to act selflessly and to help others. Love and compassion are invincible forces that bring people together, break down barriers, and create a sense of unity and community.

The Importance of Selfless Service

Amma's words also stress the importance of selfless service, in which we help others without any expectation of recognition or reward. It is a way of putting others' needs before our own and contributing to the greater good.

Applying in Daily Life

We can apply Amma's teachings of interconnectedness, love, compassion, and selfless service in many ways. We can strive to treat others with kindness and compassion, even in difficult situations. We can also look for opportunities to help others whenever we see a need.

Conclusion

Amma's quote, "We are all beads strung together on the same thread of love" is a powerful reminder of the interconnectedness of all beings and the importance of love, compassion, and selfless service. By embodying these qualities in our daily lives, together we can bring more love and compassion into the world.

***

109. Spirituality

"Spirituality is not an escape from life. It is a choice to turn inwards so that we may know ourselves. Spirituality is the science that teaches us to understand life in greater depth. It is management of the mind." – Amma

Spiritual life is a journey that many people undertake to understand their purpose in the world. It is a quest to connect with something beyond the physical realm and to explore the mysteries of the universe. For some, this journey leads them to join an ashram or community of like-minded individuals who are seeking to live a life of service and devotion. Unfortunately, this decision may not always be understood or supported by family and friends, who may have different beliefs or expectations for their loved ones. In these situations, seeking guidance and wisdom from spiritual teachers like Amma can provide clarity and insight.

Amma: Welcome, my dear ones. What brings you here today?

Father: Amma, our child has joined your ashram without our permission. We are worried about his future and want him to come back home.

Amma: I understand your concern, but your child is an adult who has made his own decision. He is on a spiritual journey and has chosen this path for a reason.

Mother: Amma, we are concerned that he is trying to escape from reality and run away from his problems.

Amma: Spirituality is not an escape from life, my dear one. It is a way to turn inward and understand oneself better. It is a science that teaches one to manage the mind and understand life in greater depth. Your son is not running away from problems, but rather learning how to face them from a higher perspective.

Mother: But Amma, we miss our son and want him back home. Can't you convince him to come back?

Amma: My dear one, I cannot force anyone to do something they do not want to do, but I can assure you that your son is in good hands and is learning valuable lessons that will benefit him in the long run. Instead of worrying, I suggest that you lend him your love and support.

Father: It is not easy, but we understand. We will do our best to support him from afar.

Amma: That is the best approach, my children.

Commentary

As a spiritual leader, Amma emphasizes the importance of spirituality in our daily lives. She clearly and consistently teaches that spirituality is not an escape from life but a way to understand and manage our lives from a deeper level.

Self-Knowledge

Spirituality is not about escaping from life, but about turning inward to know ourselves. Through spiritual practices, we can learn to understand our true nature and become more self-aware. This knowledge will help us to navigate life's challenges with skill and focus.

Understanding Life

By cultivating spiritual awareness, we can gain insights into the nature of existence, the purpose of our lives, and the interconnectedness of all things. This understanding can help us to make better decisions and make us victorious in the game of life.

Mind Management

Amma teaches that spirituality is about managing the mind. By developing a deeper understanding of ourselves and the world around us, we can learn to manage our thoughts, emotions, and actions more effectively. This, in turn, can lead to greater peace, happiness, and well-being.

Conclusion

Amma's teachings on spirituality emphasize the importance of turning inward to know ourselves, understanding life more deeply, and managing our minds effectively.

***

May Amma's grace bless to imbibe and embody her teachings in our day to day life.

Om Amritseshwaryai Namah.

Glossary

Amma: A spiritual leader and unparalleled humanitarian known for her teachings on love, compassion, and selfless service.

Bhakti: Devotion or love for the Divine, often expressed through prayer, worship, and surrender.

Brahmachari: A sincere spiritual seeker, who is observing celibacy.

Dharma: One's duty or role in life, as determined by one's nature and position in society.

Enlightenment: The state of complete liberation from the cycle of birth and death, where one realizes the true nature of reality and the eternal, infinite Self.

Guru: A spiritual teacher or guide who helps lead the student towards enlightenment and liberation.

Jnana: Spiritual knowledge or wisdom, often acquired through study and contemplation of sacred texts and teachings.

Karma: The law of cause and effect, where one's actions and intentions have consequences that determine one's future experiences.

Mantra: A sacred sound, word, or phrase repeated during meditation or prayer as a means of focusing the mind and connecting with the Divine.

Maya: The illusory nature of the material world, which obscures the true nature of reality.

Sadhana: A spiritual practice or discipline aimed at achieving spiritual growth and enlightenment.

Satsang: Gathering of like-minded individuals for the purpose of spiritual discussion, meditation, and practice.

Self-realization: The realization of one's true nature as the eternal, infinite Self, beyond the limitations of the body and mind.

Seva: Selfless service performed without any expectation of personal gain or recognition.

Yoga: A spiritual practice that aims to unite the individual soul with the Universal Soul through physical postures, breath control, and meditation.

Vedanta: A school of Hindu philosophy that emphasizes the non-dual nature of reality and the unity of the individual soul with the Universal Soul.

Frequently Asked Questions

Q: What is spirituality? A: Spirituality is the search for meaning, purpose, and connection to something greater than oneself. It involves exploring the inner world of thoughts, feelings, and beliefs, and cultivating a sense of inner peace and fulfillment.

Q: Who is Amma? A: Amma, also known as Mata Amritanandamayi, is a spiritual leader and humanitarian from India. She is renowned for her teachings on love, compassion, and selfless service, and has dedicated her life to helping others.

Q: What are Amma's teachings? A: Amma's teachings emphasize the importance of love, compassion, and selfless service. She teaches that by serving others, we can awaken our innate capacity for love and compassion and experience a deeper sense of fulfillment and purpose in life.

Q: What is selfless service? A: Selfless service, also known as seva, is the practice of serving others without expecting anything in return. It is a central practice in many spiritual traditions.

Q: How can I practice selfless service? A: You can practice selfless service in many ways, such as volunteering at a local charity or community organization, helping a friend or family member in need, or simply performing acts of kindness and compassion in your daily life.

Q: How can I find inner peace? A: Finding inner peace requires cultivating a sense of mindfulness and awareness, and learning to let go of negative thoughts and emotions. Practices such as meditation, yoga, and prayer can help you connect with your inner self and find a sense of inner peace.

Q: What is the goal of spirituality? A: The goal of spirituality is to awaken to our true nature and connect with a higher power, or universal consciousness. This connection can bring greater meaning, purpose, fulfillment and compassion into our lives.

Brief Biography of Amma

Amma, also known as Mata Amritanandamayi, was born on September 27, 1953, in a small fishing village in Kerala, India. From a young age, she displayed an extraordinary sense of compassion and a deep desire to help those in need. As a child, she would often give away her family's food and clothing to those less fortunate.

At the age of 22, Amma began to attract devotees, who were drawn by her profound love and wisdom. Over time, her following grew, and she began to travel throughout India and eventually the world, spreading her message of selfless service, love, and compassion.

In 1987, Amma founded the Mata Amritanandamayi Math, a humanitarian organization that has since grown to become one of the largest charitable organizations in India. Through the Math, Amma has established numerous hospitals, schools, and orphanages, and has provided aid to millions of people affected by natural disasters and other crises.

Today, Amma is widely regarded as one of the world's most revered spiritual leaders. Her teachings emphasize the importance of selfless service, the power of love and compassion, and the ultimate goal of realizing one's true nature as the Divine Self.

Amma's ashrams and centers are located in various countries around the world, and they offer a range of programs and activities for spiritual seekers and those interested in humanitarian work.

Some of Amma's ashrams and centers

- Amritapuri Ashram: located in Kerala, India, Amritapuri is Amma's main ashram and the headquarters of her humanitarian organization Embracing the World. The ashram is home to a large community of devotees and volunteers, and it offers a wide range of programs and activities, including daily meditation and chanting, yoga classes, and humanitarian projects such as free medical camps and disaster relief efforts. www.amritapuri.org
- Amma Center of New Mexico: located in Santa Fe, New Mexico, this center offers regular satsangs (spiritual gatherings), meditation and yoga classes, and volunteer opportunities. It also hosts special events such as retreats and workshops.
- Amma Center of Michigan: located in Ann Arbor, Michigan, this center offers weekly satsangs, meditation and yoga classes, and seva (selfless service) opportunities. It also hosts special events such as talks by visiting spiritual teachers and workshops on topics such as meditation and Ayurveda.
- Amma Center of Europe: located in Hof Herrenberg, Germany, this center offers regular satsangs, meditation and yoga classes, and volunteer opportunities. It also hosts special events such as retreats and workshops on topics such as conscious living and sustainable agriculture.

To find more information about Amma's ashrams and centers, including locations and contact details, you can visit the American website www.amma.org

How to connect with Amma

To connect with Amma and experience her loving presence, there are several ways to get involved in her global community:

1. Attend Amma's Programs: Amma travels around the world and holds programs in various cities, where she gives darshan (in the form of a loving embrace), delivers spiritual discourses, and leads devotional singing. To attend one of her programs, check her schedule on the official Amma website www.amritapuri.org and register for the event.

2. Visit Amma's Ashrams: Amma has ashrams and centers located around the world where devotees can visit, stay, and participate in spiritual practices and service activities. Check the official website of Amma for information about the locations of ashrams and centers and their schedules.

3. Participate in Seva: Amma's humanitarian organization, Embracing the World, provides opportunities for selfless service and volunteer work in various fields such as disaster relief, education, healthcare, and environmental conservation. Check the official website of Embracing the World to learn more about how to participate in seva activities.

4. Connect Online: Amma's teachings and discourses are available on Amma's official website and on social media platforms. You can also join online satsangs and meditations conducted by Amma or her disciples.

5. Contact Amma's Centers: If you have any queries or wish to connect with Amma's centers or ashrams, you can contact them directly through email, phone, or social media.

Connecting with Amma is a beautiful and transformative experience that can deepen one's spiritual journey and inspire a life of selfless service and love.

www.ingramcontent.com/pod-product-compliance
Lightning Source LLC
Chambersburg PA
CBHW071205090426
42736CB00014B/2723